# An Affair to Remember

## RECIPES, MENUS, AND HOME-ENTERTAINING TIPS FROM HOLLYWOOD'S LEADING CATERERS

### By Judy Kessler

Food Photography by Mark Elkins

For Leida
For Sid

Publisher: *W. Quay Hays*
Editorial Director: *Peter L. Hoffman*
Editor: *Dana Stibor*
Art Director: *Chitra Sekhar*
Production Director: *Trudihope Schlomowitz*
Prepress Manager: *Bill Castillo*
Production Artists: *Gaston Moraga, Bill Neary*
Production Assistants: *Tom Archibeque, David Chadderdon, Russel Lockwood*
Food Stylist: *Norman Stewart*
Copy Editor: *Catherine Cambron*

*For information:*
General Publishing Group, Inc.
2701 Ocean Park Boulevard, Suite 140
Santa Monica, CA 90405

Library of Congress Cataloging-in-Publication Data

Kessler, Judy, 1947-
    An affair to remember : recipes, menus, and home-entertaining tips
    from Hollywood's leading caterers / by Judy Kessler.
          p.    cm.
    ISBN 1-57544-082-2 (hc)
    1. Entertaining.   2. Cookery.   3. Menus.   4. Caterers and
    catering—California—Los Angeles.      I. Title.
    TX731.K46  1998                          98-7313
    642'.4—dc21                         CIP

Printed in the USA by RR Donnelley and Sons Company
10 9 8 7 6 5 4 3 2 1

General Publishing Group
*Los Angeles*

# Acknowledgments

This book has been a truly collaborative effort. It could not have been done without the extraordinary contributions of photographer Mark Elkins and food stylist Norman Stewart, for whom *An Affair to Remember* has been a labor of love. Both of them gave of their time, talent, and souls far more than any of us anticipated when we began working together, and I am indebted to them.

On the editorial side, thanks to Peter Hoffman and Dana Stibor; and to Chitra Sekhar, who is both inspired and inspirational.

Another invaluable link in the chain that has become this book is Beverly Hills' unique and wonderful store Tesoro, which supplied us endlessly with the stunning settings we used for many of our food shots. Special thanks go to store owners Tara and Marlene Riceberg and their delightful and helpful staff, Kelly Tollin, Ilpas Fiacca, and Xenia Lopez.

Deepest thanks also to Annie Glass for other glassware and settings and to Mark's Garden for many of the outstanding floral designs.

And in the realm of photography, heartfelt gratitude to assistant photographer Daniel Scott, whose technical knowledge and attention to detail helped assure the overall quality of the images presented in this book; photographic assistant, grip, and financier David Pelton, whose selfless efforts did not go unnoticed; Steve Mrozowski of Bel Air Camera's rental department, whose cooperation was key to the finished product; Kerry Morris at Samy's Camera Rental in Venice, who helped enormously; and Curt Grosjean and Sue Weinsoff at The Darkroom Lab, whose high-quality work is reflected in these pages.

Last, but certainly by no means least, I would like to thank the talented caterers who grace the pages of this book. In their typical style of giving, they were involved in this project from beginning to end, and ultimately it is their talent, skill, and unstinting cooperation that made this book possible.

# Table of Contents

# Introduction

Hollywood catering is a unique art, influenced and nurtured by the industry of the town that surrounds it: the entertainment industry. Like producing a film, a TV show, or a play, catering an event in Hollywood means many things: planning every detail from the concept, the theme, and the menu, to the design, the lighting, the decor, the music, and even the invitations. All must be harmoniously orchestrated to perfection with a creative, consistent, integrated style. That is what makes a fabulous, unforgettable party—whether for two people or two thousand.

Each caterer whom you will get to know in this book has a singular style, a distinctive trademark that sets him or her apart. Still, they all have one thing in common—talent—the talent it takes to create something few people would not want to have: an affair to remember.

In the following pages, these caterers will share their secrets. You will learn exactly how they do what they do, and how you too can accomplish this goal, from the moment the first glimmer of the event enters your mind to the moment your guests go home. You will learn how to plan, organize, shop, cook, decorate, and light. With the components it takes to create a total ambience you too will have the ability to create a wonderful party. And perhaps even more important, you'll be able to enjoy the party along with the rest of your guests, using the insiders' "tricks of the trade," Hollywood's best-kept catering secrets.

So dig in, devour, digest, and enjoy. You're guaranteed to be satisfied when you are done. You'll be left not with an empty plate, but with something that is sure to last forever: the ability to entertain with the style, flair, grace, warmth, and savoir faire of Hollywood's top catering experts; and the capacity to have an affair to remember.

# ALONG CAME MARY

## Mary Micucci

It is so exciting to establish new parameters, set a style, a tone, a level of expectation. As event producers, we create once-in-a-lifetime experiences by combining technical wizardry, leading-edge decor, and unique entertainment. But my personal passion is food. I understand its importance, the beauty of it, the brilliance of it. The perfect combination of all these elements is what makes an event unforgettably spectacular.

# The Affair

## The *Men in Black* Premiere Party

A deep, eerie rumbling filled the air, and clouds of mysterious, hazy smoke enveloped the immense dome-like object. Tiny beaming lights encompassed its girth and it appeared to be spinning, coming to a stop as though it had just landed. A UFO if there ever was one. Aliens, for sure. Letters were detectable now as the smoke abated, bright neon letters, easy to make out: M-I-B.

*Men in Black.*

It appeared as though people were alighting from the spaceship. There was Will Smith. Jada Pinkett. Tommy Lee Jones. Was it a scene from the movie?

Not quite. It was the beginning of the dazzling premiere party, created and produced by Along Came Mary, whose mastermind, Mary Micucci, is Hollywood's undisputed reigning catering queen. For more than 20 years, her magic touch and her unequaled creative vision have transformed the very concept of the movie premiere party from that of a glamorous but traditional soiree to a Hollywood production as detailed, nuanced, and exciting as the movie itself.

The spaceship was the kickoff to the *Men in Black* party and the result of the Micucci team's six-month search, with Columbia TriStar Motion Pictures, for the consummate party site. Their final decision? The spheroid Hollywood icon of architecture, the Cinerama Dome (with its adjacent 150,000-square-foot parking lot), which Micucci the visionary and her corps perceived as the perfect spaceship, and the perfect backdrop to a party based on a movie about UFOs, aliens, and the Men in Black, whose mission it was to keep the aliens in check. By the time Micucci's inspired concept was executed, it was clear that she was correct.

As guests left the Cinerama Dome theater that night through the misty smoke wafting stealthily around them, it really appeared as though they were exiting a UFO: the low hum of the ship's engine pulsing, lights spinning, aliens joining the guests as they exited the theater. All proceeded along a plush black carpet that led elegantly to what had been, only days ago, the immense parking lot, miraculously transformed now into a scene from the movie: Command Central, otherwise known as I.N.S. Division 6, the headquarters for the Men in Black, through which aliens were required to pass before descending upon planet Earth.

Within the walls of the open-air tent, reality and fantasy merged completely. An alien stood in a booth handing out *Men in Black* Ray-Ban sunglasses. A warning sign flashed: PUT ON SUN-GLASSES NOW. Sunglasses were the only protection from the rays utilized to zap the memory of humans who had encountered aliens. As guests proceeded further down the entrance corridor, announcements echoed around them in various galactic languages. When guests entered the main event area, high-tech multimedia trusses and lighting towered around them. A stunning futuristic dance floor overflowed with "well-behaved" aliens dancing with partygoers, while giant screens surrounding them flashed their images surrealistically. At one end of the tent, a disc jockey spun records. At the other, "The Gravitron," a breathtaking spaceship-shaped carnival ride, spun guests. As the bottom dropped from the ride, the force of gravity kept them fastened to the wall like magnets, conveying a thrilling and real sense of the weightlessness of space. Everywhere you turned was another visual treat, another reminder of a scene from the film, another activity, another surprise.

Consistent with Micucci's philosophy, the food was no less spectacular than the event, thanks in a large part to her longtime executive chef, Billy Starbuck, lauded as one of the top catering chefs on the West Coast. In contrast to the high-tech setting, the menu was solid American comfort food. Waiters moved about the stylized white Lycra-draped tables and chairs in the official MIB uniforms of white shirts, white ties, black jackets—and the requisite Ray-Bans—serving the specialty drink of the night: Martian Mango Margaritas. On the tables, the centerpieces were neon Saturn rings; metal and glass buffet tables were lit from below, illuminating the food with an ethereal glow.

Among the dishes were soft-shell crabs with crispy Belgian sweet and Russet potato fries and beer-battered onion rings. Burgers were a big hit—but not your everyday, run-of-the-mill hamburgers. Here you could find a seafood burger with shrimp, crab, and lobster, along with turkey burgers and lamb burgers, accompanied by traditional toppings with a twist: rhubarb ketchup, sundried tomato tartar sauce, and cucumber tomato mint salsa. Desserts included familiar favorites with a universal flair: rich chocolate truffle cake, tangy key lime napoleons, succulent apple tarts, a summer ice cream sundae bar, and a wonderful summer fruit soup topped with pear ginger granita.

Guests partied until the MIB police pulled the plug, satiated finally with the abundant supplies of food, fun, and excitement. It was another illustrious Along Came Mary affair, but that was to be expected. As Deborah Rosen of Universal Studios explains, "I've been working alongside Mary for 15 years, and each time out we have somehow outdone ourselves with the type, the scope, the style. Nobody can do a premiere party like Mary Micucci. She is really out of this world."

# Men in Black: The Premiere Party Full Menu

Created especially for Columbia Pictures'
*Men in Black* premiere, June 25, 1997

Partial Menu

## OUT OF THIS WORLD STATIONS

**INS Division #6 Flavors**

## Performance Soft-Shell Crab

Maryland crabs dredged in flour then sautéed in a touch of butter with lemon, garlic, olive oil, and
Italian parsley; served with

## Sun-dried Tomato Tartar Sauce

## Roasted Corn Onion Relish

## Herb Oil Vinaigrette

## Belgian Sweet & Russet Potato Fries

Golden potato spears baked with skins and ultra crispy Belgian-style fries
lightly dusted with sea salt and served with rhubarb ketchup

## Grilled Artichoke & Tomato Salad

Grilled artichokes layered with red and yellow tomato slices,
all drizzled with a light citrus vinaigrette and garnished with orange zest curls

## Classic Coleslaw

Tricolored cabbage tossed with shredded carrots and a creamy caraway dressing

**Alien Grille**

# Butterflied Leg of Lamb

Butterflied leg of lamb rubbed with Dijon mustard and fresh thyme and grilled to perfection;
performance-sliced and served on

# Rosemary Herb Focaccia

with

# Warm Mint Glacé de Viande

# Stilton Creme Fraiche

# Roasted Tomato Mint Relish

# Skewered Rosemary Prawns

Succulent jumbo prawns marinated in lemon, rosemary, and extra virgin olive oil, garnished with
crispy beet chips and served with Italian parsley gazpacho sauce,
on a bed of
classic mashed potatoes (russet potatoes whipped light and fluffy, flavored with
sweet cream and a touch of butter)

# Roasted Peppers & Feta

Roasted red bell peppers brushed with extra virgin olive oil and topped with
crumbled feta cheese, oregano, and cracked pepper

## "Old Guys" Gourmet Burgers

## Sirloin Burgers

100% ground sirloin served on a mini sesame onion bun with choice of Vermont cheddar cheese, grilled pancetta strips, Bermuda onion relish, wild mushroom sauté, rhubarb ketchup, lemon parsley horseradish mustard, sun-dried tomato mustard, roma tomatoes, and red leaf lettuce

## Turkey Burgers

100% ground turkey served on a honey sunflower mini bun with choice of Jarlsberg Swiss cheese, roasted red and yellow peppers, sautéed sweet onions, bourbon molasses mustard, whole grain mustard, and sprouts

## Seafood Frita Burger

A savory blend of scallops and shrimp grilled to perfection and served on a sesame seed bun with classic remoulade, butter lettuce, and sliced sweet yellow tomatoes

## Falafel Burgers

A vegetarian delight served on whole wheat pita with choice of dill yogurt sauce, tahini dressing, Greek salad relish, crumbled feta, and roasted peppers

with

## Sweet Onion Rings

Sweet Vidalia onions coated with homemade batter and bread crumbs, then fried golden

## Crispy Chips

Homemade beet parsnip and yam potato chips fried until crisp, then lightly dusted with sea salt

## Antipasti

# Melon & Prosciutto
Sweet juicy melon wrapped in paper-thin slices of Italian ham

# Grilled Radicchio, Japanese Eggplant & Zucchini
Wrapped in pancetta and drizzled with a creamy parsley vinaigrette

# Buffalo Mozzarella Skewers
Skewered with roma tomatoes and drizzled with extra virgin olive oil

# Fried Calamari
Fresh squid dipped in a lightly seasoned batter then fried until golden,
served with aioli and lemon wedges

# Frisée Salad
Tossed with a light citrus vinaigrette and topped with crispy matchstick potatoes

# Italian Breads
Herb Crostini, Ciabatta, Kalamata Olive Bread

served with

# Extra Virgin Olive Oil
# Tomato Coulis

## Undercover Desserts

### Summer Sundae Bar
Create your own classic with fresh summer flavors

### Fresh Peach Ice Cream, Strawberry Ice Cream, Coconut Ice Cream
served with

### Passion Fruit Soup
A blend of passion fruit and summer fruits garnished with crème fraîche and Ginger Pear Granita

### Chocolate Bread Pudding
Old fashioned bread pudding with a twist; served with a crème Anglaise
with a hot berry compote

### Key Lime Napoleons
Delicate wafers layered with key lime creme, garnished with candied lime slices,
and topped with whipped cream

### Apple Tart Tartin
A mini buttery crust brimming with cinnamon-flavored baked apples;
garnished with a miniature ice cream cone filled with vanilla bean ice cream

### Almond Tulipe
A delicate almond-flavored tulipe shell filled with Chantilly Cream & fresh summer berries

#### Minis

### Lemon Meringue Tart, Peanut Butter Pies, Pecan Squares

### A Selection of Along Came Mary Cookies
### French Roast Coffee Service

# The Recipes

## Artichoke & Soft-shell Crab Salad
(SERVES 4)

| | |
|---|---|
| 4 soft-shell crabs | Salt and white pepper |
| ¾ cup flour | 4 large artichoke bottoms |
| ½ tsp. ground chili powder | 2 yellow tomatoes |
| 2 Tbs. sesame seeds | 2 red tomatoes |
| ½ tsp. paprika | I bunch fresh basil |
| I egg | ¼ cup extra virgin olive oil |
| ¼ cup grapeseed oil | Salt and black pepper |

Boil artichokes until al dente. Remove leaves and choke and set aside. Brush with olive oil, salt, and black pepper. Slice tomatoes into thick slices and brush with olive oil, salt, and black pepper. Grill all items 1—2 minutes on grill.

Place flour, chili powder, sesame seeds, and paprika in small bowl. Season with salt and white pepper. Put egg in separate bowl. Lightly dust the soft-shell crabs with regular flour. Dip crabs in egg and then lightly dust with sesame seeds and flour mixture.

Cook crabs in grapeseed oil in very hot pan, about 2 minutes on each side. Remove from pan and drain on paper towels.

## Sun-dried Tomato Tartar Sauce
(YIELD: 1/2 CUP)

2 Tbs. pureed sun-dried tomatoes

1/2 cup mayonnaise

Sesame seeds to taste

Mix sun-dried tomatoes in mayonnaise and sesame seeds to taste.

## Roasted Corn Onion Relish
(YIELD: 2 CUPS)

| | |
|---|---|
| 1 ear white corn | 2 Tbs. avocado or olive oil |
| 1/4 cup diced red onion | 1 tsp. thyme |
| 1 Tbs. cider vinegar | Salt and black pepper |

Grill and de-cob corn, finely dice red onion, and mix with vinegar, oil, thyme, salt, and pepper.

## Herb Oil Vinaigrette
(YIELD: 1/2 CUP)

| | |
|---|---|
| 1 1/2 Tbs. herb vinegar | 1/2 tsp. chopped garlic |
| 6 1/2 Tbs. extra virgin olive oil | Salt and pepper |

Mix all items together until well blended.

TO ASSEMBLE: Drizzle plate with tartar sauce. Place artichoke bottoms in center of plate, then put basil leaves between alternating layers of red and yellow tomatoes. Place crab on top, drizzle vinaigrette around plate, and sprinkle with corn relish.

## Skewered Rosemary Prawns
(SERVES 4)

12 large shrimp

12 sprigs rosemary

¼ cup extra virgin olive oil

2 Tbs. chopped Italian parsley

Zest of ½ lemon

Chop parsley and zest and mix with olive oil. Coat shrimp and skewer with rosemary sprigs. Grill for 3-5 minutes.

## Beet Chips

1 large beet

Slice beet ¹/₂ inch thick and cut into squares. Fry in soy oil until crispy.

## Mashed Potatoes

| | |
|---|---|
| 4 potatoes | ½ cup melted butter |
| ½ cup cream | Salt and pepper |

Peel and cube potatoes and boil until tender. Mash until smooth, adding cream and melted butter. Season with salt and pepper to taste.

## Garnish

1 sprig Italian parsley

## Gazpacho Sauce

(1 CUP)

| | |
|---|---|
| 3 roma tomatoes | ½ tsp. garlic |
| ¼ cup red bell peppers | 1 tsp. lemon juice |
| ¼ cup diced cucumber | Salt and white pepper |
| 1 Tbs. chopped red onion | |

Seed and chunk tomatoes, peppers, and cucumbers. Puree all ingredients until smooth. Season with salt and white pepper and push through fine sieve.

*Mary's Tips*

The key element of a party is that

guests feel comfortable.

TO ASSEMBLE: Make a cylinder of mashed potatoes in the center of the plate. Put a quarter of the julienne potatoes on top of the mashed potatoes, then lean grilled shrimp skewers against the potatoes and place on beet chips. Lightly warm the sauce, drizzle between the shrimp, and garnish with parsley leaves.

## Frisée Salad
(SERVES 4)

1 lb. baby frisée

### Citrus Vinaigrette
½ cup olive oil

¼ cup champagne vinegar

3 Tbs. grated orange zest

Whisk all vinaigrette items together. Wash and dry frizee. Thinly slice onion rings, dredge in seasoned flour, and golden fry in soy oil. Lightly dress frizee and top with onion rings.

# Apple Tart Tartin
(SERVES 12)

**Tart Tartin**

14 red delicious apples

2 Tbs. unsalted butter

1 cup granulated sugar

½ cup water

12 oz. puff pastry sheet (circle—should be baked before tart tartins)

Peel apples and reserve in lemon water. Arrange stainless steel rings (3" x 2 ¼" or 2" x 2" for mini size; for mini size, use half the amount of apples and split the recipe in half). Caramelize sugar with butter and water. When amber color, pour into non-stick tart pans ½ inch larger than the ring mold being used. Caramel should be ¹⁄₁₆ inch thick.

Slice each apple into thin slivers (¹⁄₁₆ inch thick), keeping the shape of the apple. Press each apple into mold, discarding the excess. When all molds are prepped, put trays in oven and bake at 350° for 15 minutes. Apple will appear translucent.

Roll puff pastry sheet out ¹⁄₁₆ inch and cut (3" x 2 ¼" or 2" x 2") circles out of dough. Place circles on sheet trays with parchment paper and bake at 400°. Circles are ready when light brown.

Place baked circles atop apple tarts inside ring and return to oven for 15 minutes. Remove tarts from oven and cool slightly. Invert tarts and slip out of rings into palm, being careful not to burn fingers with excess caramel. Reserve caramel to sauce plates. Put tarts on parchment paper—lined trays. Cool.

## Almond Florentine Cone

1 cup florentina mix

2 cup natural almonds, blanched and sliced

½ cup all-purpose flour

Mix all ingredients. Prepare parchment paper—lined tray. With small ice cream scoop, scoop dough and place mounds at 3-inch intervals on sheet tray. Press down while making perfect circles.

Place tray in oven and bake at 350° until light golden brown. Remove from oven and slide paper onto cool surface. With the edge of a metal spatula quickly slide underneath each round to loosen from paper. Cut each round in half.

Pick up halves and roll piece around finger to form closed end cones. Repeat until you have 12 cones. Store in shallow container and put in cool place until ready to use.

## Praline

1 cup almonds, sliced and toasted

½ cup granulated sugar

¼ cup water

Heat sugar and water in a heavy saucepan. When color changes to amber, add nuts to caramel, stir and pour into sheet tray. Cool until hard. Crumble with knife into small pieces. Reserve in cup.

## Mary's Tips

Know your audience, and make choices with them in mind; It's not just about what you want to do.

## Mary's Tips

To Assemble: Sauce 12 plates with reserved caramel in a free-form design. Place praline pieces around plate. Put tarts in the center of plates. Stick cones into centers of tarts. With 1-inch wide ice cream disher, scoop cream into 1 ½-inch balls, place in cones, sprinkle tops of tarts with excess praline. Garnish with mint leaves.

## Almond Tulipe

### Almond Tulipe Shell

2 cups florentina mix

1 cup almonds, blanched and sliced

¼ cup all-purpose flour

Mix all ingredients in mixer with bowl attachment. Prepare parchment-lined tray. Scoop mounds of dough 1-inch wide onto trays. Press down, forming 12 perfect circles. Place tray in oven at 350°. Bake for 15 minutes or until light golden brown.

Remove from oven and slide paper from tray onto cool surface. Working quickly, slip metal spatula underneath cookies and release from paper. Form cups with fluted edges around the bottoms of 8-ounce glasses. Store cups on tray in cool place until ready to use.

## Chantilly Cream

4 cups heavy cream          ¼ cup sugar

4 egg yolks                 Vanilla bean

¼ cup milk

Heat milk until it scalds. In medium mixing bowl whisk eggs and sugar together. Pour half of milk into bowl and pour mix back into pot. With wooden spoon, stir mixture until it thickens and coats spoon. Remove from heat, strain into clean bowl and chill custard in refrigerator. Whip cream in mixer bowl until thick. Slice one vanilla bean in half lengthwise, scoop out pulp, and add to cream. Stir until thoroughly mixed. Fold custard into cream. Chill for one hour or until very firm.

## Raspberry Sauce

3 baskets red raspberries

4 Tbs. sugar

12 sprigs mint

Add 2 baskets of raspberries and sugar to food processor bowl fitted with blade. Process until sauce is smooth. Strain sauce into bowl. Refrigerate to chill.

TO ASSEMBLE: Sauce 12 plates with dots of raspberry sauce. Place cups in center of plate.

With star tip—fitted pastry bag, fill with cream. Pipe a rosette mound into each cup. Garnish with remaining berries and mint.

Billy Starbuck

# Key Lime Napoleons

### Key Lime Curd

2 cups key lime juice

7 egg yolks

5 whole eggs

3 cups granulated sugar

1 Tbs. gelatin, powdered

½ cup water

2 limes, zested, chopped fine

Preheat oven to 400°. Flour work surface. Place puff pastry sheet atop and sprinkle a little flour over top of dough. Pull sheet in all directions to a ¹⁄₁₆-inch thickness. Cut dough into 3-inch triangles and place onto parchment paper—lined baking sheet at 7-inch intervals. Continue with other sheets. Brush triangles with water and sprinkle with sugar. Put sheet trays on top rack of oven and bake until golden brown.*

Remove tray(s) from oven and cool on rack.

*If dough rises above ¼ inch, remove tray(s) from oven, place fitted parchment paper sheet over triangles, and place another baking sheet into bottom tray. Put back in oven and continue baking.

### Whipped Cream

1 cup whipping cream

3 Tbs. granulated sugar

1 tsp. vanilla extract

Pour cream into a chilled small mixer bowl. Add sugar and vanilla, and whip until cream is thick and fluffy.

## A Small Sampling of Along Came Mary's Premieres

AIR FORCE ONE

BATMAN

BEVERLY HILLS COP II

BIG

BRAVEHEART

EMPIRE OF THE SUN

FORREST GUMP

THE FUGITIVE

GREASE II

HOOK

INDIANA JONES AND THE LAST
  CRUSADE

INDIANA JONES AND THE TEMPLE
  OF DOOM

INTERVIEW WITH THE VAMPIRE

JUMANJI

MEN IN BLACK

MISSION IMPOSSIBLE

MRS. DOUBTFIRE

### Raspberry Coulis

1 basket red raspberries

Push berries through fine sieve and reserve juice.

### Puff Pastry Triangles

3 12 oz. puff pastry shells

2 Tbs. granulated sugar

¼ cup water

¼ cup flour

### Vanilla Sauce

3 cups homogenized milk

¼ cup granulated sugar

8 egg yolks

1 vanilla bean, split

Heat milk in heavy saucepan until it just begins to scald. Break yolks into a bowl and whisk in sugar. Cut vanilla bean, scoop out pulp, and add to egg mixture. Pour half of milk into egg mixture, whisk thoroughly, add back to milk, and stir with wooden spoon until sauce begins to thicken. Remove from stove top, strain through china paper and chill over ice.

### Key Lime Sauce

1 cup reserved key lime curd

¼ cup key lime juice

2 key limes, zested, chopped fine

Put reserved lime curd into stainless steel bowl, whisk in lime juice to thin. Sprinkle zest over mixture and stir thoroughly.

## Candied Key Lime Peel

12 key limes

¼ cup granulated sugar

With citrus peeler, carefully cut elongated strip, beginning at top of lime and ending at bottom. Sprinkle with sugar and place strips on parchment-lined trays and place in an off oven slightly ajar for 2 hours or until zest becomes crispy.

Remove from oven and let air dry a little longer.

OTHER INGREDIENTS:

2 blood oranges

Powdered sugar

TO ASSEMBLE: Sprinkle powdered sugar over puff pastry triangles. Fit pastry bag with lime curd. Set up triangles (24) all in one direction.

Pipe rosettes the length of the triangles. Build the napoleons, stacking the second triangle at a 25° angle. The third triangle stacks at a 25° angle. Fit another pastry bag with whipped cream. Reserve.

Sauce plates covering the base with lime sauce. Dot vanilla sauce with a spoon at the four corners of the plate. Dot raspberry coulis above vanilla sauce at the four corners. Segment blood oranges and drain excess juice on paper towel. Place 4 segments between dotted sauces.

Arrange each stack of two triangles in center of sauced plates, fitting the third puff pastry triangle at a 25° angle. Pipe whipped cream atop each third-layer triangle and stick lime decor into cream at an upward angle.

Mary Micucci

# COLIN COWIE LIFESTYLE

## *Colin Cowie*

"I LOOK AT EVERYTHING AS AN EXPERIENCE. It must have a definite beginning, a middle, and an end, and there must always be an element of surprise. I appeal to all the senses—sight, sound, touch, and taste—in everything I do. But the most important aspect is timing, and it doesn't cost a dime."

# The Affair

## A Wedding Anniversary Party at the Beach

He has been dubbed a "mod, bicoastal version of Martha Stewart" and "the King of Catering." But the elegantly simple, singular style that most accurately defines Colin Cowie truly defies comparison. With his two recently published books, *Effortless Elegance with Colin Cowie* and *Colin Cowie Weddings*, along with a new line of china Cowie designed for Lenox, and even greater plans for the future (which include his own magazine and a line of Colin Cowie furniture), he is fast becoming an industry in his own right.

Everything that bears Cowie's touch—from the food to the decor, from the music to the lighting, from the flowers to the choice of wines to the dessert, down to the scale of the glass, even the amount of starch in the napkin—underscores his extraordinary ability to attain an ideal combination of warmth, simplicity, and exquisite taste. "My work is about quality," explains Cowie. "The bottom line of entertaining is that there are no rules, but that style should prevail abundantly."

His philosophy could not have been better exemplified than it was at the recent wedding anniversary party Cowie did for two well-known clients at their home at Carbon Beach in Malibu, California. As usual, his work began with the development of a concept. "I try to get a window into their soul and to find out what type of image they want to project, who they are, their sense of style, and the objective of the evening," explains Cowie, "because invariably people want to project a particular type of style and we will use many tools—flowers, music, lighting—to create that particular ambience and that feeling."

In this case, it was one word uttered by his client that inspired Cowie. "She mentioned the word *whimsical* and that said everything to me," he recalls. "The vision dropped into my head." It was a warm, intimate, yet fanciful concept: a single long table for 40 guests, nestled under a 40-foot canopy swathed in mounds of chiffon that blew freely in the wind; well-cushioned chairs and padded tables draped with vintage white linens that flowed to the ground; big hemstitch napkins with silver napkin rings; gorgeous Lenox plates with platinum borders; and hand-inscribed place cards at each setting. The flowers were at once beautiful and whimsical: a silver urn packed with huge Ecuadorian roses, accentuated with spurts of white lily of the valley; candelabras around which masses of roses flowed into bunches of grapes, with smaller silver vases between them, again packed with white roses.

True to Cowie's style, it was elegant yet masterfully simple. "I used only white linen and white flowers throughout—white roses mainly—and I kept it very pure. I found a gorgeous vintage crystal chandelier which hung over the center of the table. For lighting, we created soft, gentle patterns, which gave a marbling effect, almost like moonlight over the table and over the top of the canopy."

When it came to the food and wine, the same theme endured. As the guests arrived to the sounds of 20 violins playing, they were handed a glass of champagne—a rare Pink Taitinger '76—and a single hors d'oeuvre: homemade brioche topped with homemade foie gras. "The client and I decided it had to be the finest of the finest," says Cowie. And it was. There were caviar, smoked salmon, truffles, lamb, foie gras, extraordinary wines. Dinner was served by waiters perfectly synchronized as they appeared simultaneously around the table with the platters and plates. The evening's entertainment included a dazzling fireworks display coordinated to music, capped by a dessert of miniature wedding cakes baked by a friend of Cowie's and flown in specially from New York.

In every sense, the evening met Colin Cowie's definition of success: "When you're able to pull it all together and get everything to work in harmony, you get that reaction, 'Isn't this divine, this is so happening, isn't this just beyond...' And it's that moment in the evening when it all comes together and everyone's had just enough cocktails and there's just enough candlelight on their skin and everyone looks fabulous, and the laughter is up and the volume is up at the table and the plates are coming back empty, and you know that it's a success."

# The Menu

### Tray-passed Appetizer

Homemade Brioche with Homemade Foie Gras Served with Champagne

### First Course

Cappuccino of Tomato

Ice-cold, lemon-scented tomato coulis topped with cream and served in a hollowed-out eggshell
with a straw

Mille-feuille of Caviar & Smoked Salmon
with Chive Sauce

### Entrée

Herbed Rack of Lamb with Bordelaise Sauce
or
Grilled John Dory with Spring Vegetables

### Salad Course

Salad with Asparagus Tips
& Artichoke Truffle Vinaigrette

### Dessert

A Miniature Handmade Wedding Cake for Each Guest

## Tips from the Guru of Style

Never let a cocktail hour last longer than 45 minutes.

Do it in a way that will allow you to do all the work in advance.

Everything has to have a sense of flow. Never let anything drag.

There must always be an element of surprise.

The whole idea about entertaining is not about impressing people but about having fun and investing quality time with them.

It's okay to get great takeout. Better to buy an exquisite torte the baker makes than to serve a mediocre one you made yourself.

It's important that, as the host,

## The Recipes

### Mille-feuille of Caviar & Smoked Salmon with Chive Sauce
(SERVES 10)

1 egg yolk

¼ lb. butter

6 sheets phyllo pastry

Sour Cream Mixture (see following recipe)

20 oz. presliced smoked salmon, cut into 20 1-oz. slices

10 oz. beluga, osetra, or sevruga caviar

¼ cup large diced red onion

Chive Sauce (see recipe below)

Preheat the oven to 450°. In a small bowl, beat the egg with 1 tablespoon of cold water, set aside. In a small saucepan, melt the butter over medium heat until white solids separate and bubble to the top. Set aside to cool, then remove and discard the foam from the top. The butter is now clarified.

Place 1 sheet of phyllo on a cutting board and lightly brush with the butter. Cover with a second sheet of phyllo, coat with more butter, and repeat with the third sheet.

With a sharp knife, cut the phyllo into 16 equal rectangles. Transfer to a baking sheet and brush with the egg wash. Bake until golden brown, about 4 minutes. Set aside to cool. Repeat the procedure with the remaining phyllo to make 32 rectangles.

Spread 1 heaping teaspoon of the Sour Cream Mixture over 10 phyllo pieces. Top with 1 slice of salmon and a dab of caviar. Top with another sheet of phyllo and repeat the sour cream, salmon, and caviar layers. Top with another piece of phyllo, a teaspoon of the Sour Cream Mixture, and caviar.

To serve, place the finished pastry in the center of each of 10 serving plates. Sprinkle the plate with the onion. Drizzle with the Chive Sauce.

## Sour Cream Mixture
(MAKES 2 CUPS)

| | |
|---|---|
| 1/2 large red onion, diced | Juice of 2 lemons |
| 16 oz. sour cream | 1/2 tsp. salt |
| 2 Tbs. thinly sliced chives | 1/8 tsp. white pepper |

In a mixing bowl, combine the red onion, sour cream, chives, lemon juice, salt, and pepper. Mix well and set aside.

## Chive Sauce
(MAKES 1/2 CUP)

| | |
|---|---|
| 1 cup heavy cream | Rind of 1/2 lemon |
| 1 bunch chives | Salt and freshly ground pepper |

Place the cream in a small saucepan and bring to a boil. Cook until reduced by half. Blanch the lemon in boiling water for 30 seconds and add to the cream. Season with salt and pepper. Transfer to a blender and add the chives. Blend until pureed and then strain through a fine sieve. Set aside or refrigerate.

you be as cool as a cucumber. Never shout, never give off nervous energy at a party. Be as calm and relaxed as any guest in the room. There's nothing stylish about seeing someone running around disheveled, looking like they're working too hard. It should always appear both effortless and elegant.

If you're entertaining at home, do something easy, like soup, salad, and a stew. It can all be prepared in advance, you can't burn the soup, the stew's already made. Make it foolproof. If it's foolproof, you've got nothing to worry about, and you can spend the extra 15 minutes on yourself.

# Herbed Rack of Lamb with Bordelaise Sauce
(SERVES 10)

| | |
|---|---|
| 1 bunch rosemary | 2 cups dry bread crumbs |
| 1 bunch thyme | 1/4 lb. butter, melted, |
| 1 medium head garlic, cloves | plus 2 Tbs. |
| separated and chopped, | Salt and freshly ground pepper |
| plus 3 to 4 cloves minced | 1 cup Dijon mustard |
| 2 Tbs. olive oil | 1 cup dry white wine |
| 4 lamb racks (1 lb. each) | 2 cups veal stock |
| 1 bunch parsley | 1 cup tomato juice |

Strip the leaves from the rosemary and thyme, and coarsely chop them. Set aside 1/4 cup of the chopped rosemary for sauce. Place the chopped herbs in a small bowl and add the chopped garlic and olive oil. Mix to blend thoroughly.

Rub the herb mixture all over the lamb racks. Arrange them in a shallow dish, cover, and refrigerate for at least 8 hours or up to 24 hours. Strip the leaves from the parsley and coarsely chop them. In a medium bowl combine the chopped parsley with the bread crumbs and melted butter. Mix to blend thoroughly and set aside.

Preheat the oven to 400°. Set a large heavy skillet over medium-high heat and add 2 tablespoons butter. When hot, add the lamb racks, two at a time, and cook for 4 to 5 minutes on each side, or until browned. Remove racks from the pan. Do not wash the pan. Sprinkle the racks with salt and pepper to taste, then brush all over with the mustard. Using your hands, press

---

## On Music

Make sure there is always some music playing. Start out with something a little lively to help the conversation at the beginning of the evening, something with a jazzy beat, like a little 1950s lounge music—something to get the feet tapping and the glasses going. Then you've inspired them—you're using everything you can energy-wise. Make the music a little louder during the cocktail hour. During dinner do something a little lower key, a little softer, a little more instrumental. But always have music, from the time the guests arrive until they leave.

## On Lighting

Dim all the lights. It costs 10 dollars for a dimmer switch. Every single switch in every home should have a dimmer so you can set the mood. Keep it subdued and light lots of candles.

Never have fluorescent lights, even in the bathroom.

Never have fragrant candles on the dinner table. There's nothing worse than smelling vanilla when you're eating lamb. But do use the fragrant candles in the bathrooms and elsewhere.

The bottom line of entertaining is that there are no rules, but that style should prevail abundantly. My definition of style doesn't have to do with the watch, the car, the shoes, but how we treat one another—with a sense of mutual respect. This paves the way for you to think very carefully about how to entertain your guests.

the reserved bread crumb mixture over the meat, leaving the bones exposed. Arrange the lamb racks in a large roasting pan and roast for 20 to 25 minutes or until desired doneness—125° for rare, 140° for medium, and 160° for well done. Remove from the oven and keep warm.

Meanwhile, set the pan with the reserved drippings over medium-high heat. Deglaze the pan with the white wine and transfer to pot. Add the stock, tomato juice, minced garlic, and reserved rosemary. Bring the mixture to a boil, then lower the heat to simmer and reduce by 3/4 (approximately 40 minutes). Whisk in the butter. Strain the sauce, and season with salt and pepper to taste. Keep warm.

Carve the lamb racks into individual chops. Stand 3 chops in the center of each warm dinner plate, creating a pyramid with the chop bones at the top. Spoon some of the sauce around the chops and surround them with the vegetables.

## Salad with Asparagus Tips & Artichoke Truffle Vinaigrette
(SERVES 10)

¼ cup lemon juice

1 Tbs. Dijon mustard

1 cooked artichoke bottom,
   quartered

½ cup truffle oil

½ cup olive oil

Salt and freshly ground pepper

1 pound mâche, frisée, or
   butter lettuce

20 asparagus tips, blanched

2 tablespoons chopped chives

In a blender, combine the lemon juice, mustard, and artichoke bottom. Process until smooth. With the blender running, gradually drizzle in the oils in a thin stream. Season to taste with salt and pepper.

In a large bowl, toss the mâche with the dressing. Pile the salad onto 12 individual salad plates. Place the asparagus tips decoratively on the front of each plate. Sprinkle with the chives.

# DC3

## Thaddeus Hunter Smith

"IT'S ALL VISUAL—THE FOOD AND THE PARTY. People eat with their eyes. The party starts when the guests get out of their cars."

# *The Affair*

## "Into The Unknown," a Fundraiser

Picture this: You are an executive at a major L.A. movie studio and you receive an invitation to a fundraiser. You wish you didn't have to go. "Oh," you say, "another boring fundraiser." Wrong!

You arrive at the party site, the Museum of Flying, which is adjacent to and owned by the posh restaurant DC3, located, of all places, at the Santa Monica Airport. You're wearing proper attire as requested: black tie. As you alight from your car at the valet, it seems as though you are stepping onto a launching pad. A Marine greets you and checks his official list to make sure you have clearance. As you step onto the plush red carpet, you spot a spaceship up ahead with a cloud of white smoke streaming from its tail, looking as if it is about to take off—and that is precisely where the carpet is leading you.

You enter the spaceship, and the countdown begins immediately. A voice booms out: "10, 9, 8...3, 2, blast off!" You look out the window, and you seem to be flying through space. You see stars and planets whizzing by, and then within moments you have landed. As you get out, two daunting, 100-foot doors part slowly, and an eerie blue fog seeps mysteriously through them. You have entered another world. When the ethereal fog enshrouding you clears, you realize you have just landed on the moon.

A lunar module picks you up, and people in strange space outfits visible in flashing bursts of light escort you to the moon station. Another low voice booms over the loudspeaker: "Please take three deep breaths, and everything will be fine; your breathing will continue as normal." Breathing is different up here, but you force yourself to breathe deeply. Could it be? You could swear you are actually on the moon.

A silent auction for the fundraiser is going on as delicious hors d'oeuvres are being passed: Grilled Shiitake Mushrooms with Sun-dried Tomato Relish; Cracked Pepper Beef Carpaccio with Roquefort Sauce; Stuffed Prawns with Fresh Spinach, Parmesan Cheese, and Garlic; Blackened Sea

Scallops on Braised Leeks with Cilantro Lime Sauce. You then sit at your table, made of silver Mylar, with blue moon rocks as centerpieces, glittering with gold, surrounded by mushroom-like plants and vines. You look up to see thousands of twinkling lights—you could swear you are looking back at Earth.

You are served dinner at your table, and it is difficult to choose between the mouthwatering Sea Bass on Pearl Pasta with a Yellow Pepper Sauce and the magnificent Charred Fillet of Beef with a Red Wine Demi Glaze. But the dessert! The Chocolate Soufflé Pie is out of this world. You sip your coffee before reentering the atmosphere for your journey back to earth.

Thaddeus Hunter Smith is the genius behind this trip to the moon as well as all the other events catered by DC3, which owns several magnificent party venues at the restaurant site, including the steel-and-glass, 53,000-square-foot, three-level Museum of Flying. Smith came to DC3 after a soaring career, beginning as a busboy, a waiter, the restaurant manager, and finally the banquet manager for the Hollywood Roosevelt Hotel before landing at DC3. For the events, he oversees the decor, the concept, the ambience, the lighting, the design of the invitation, the music—virtually every detail involved in planning and executing an affair. But he maintains that his work is not as difficult as it appears.

For the trip to the moon fundraiser, Smith used foam board and plywood to build the spaceship. "I'm building images," he stresses. "When someone has a limited budget, that's when I get the most creative." He rented a red carpet, dressed two waiters in Marine uniforms, and had a 40-foot screen on the wall that could be viewed from the spaceship, making it appear as though it were actually flying through space. The blue fog seeping through the museum's 100-foot hangar doors was created with dry ice.

"You can come really close to what I did at your own home," he insists. We had a borrowed car that looked like a lunar module car, and dressed the waiters in space outfits. They were standing in the blue fog having strobe lights hit them, and it was an awesome sight. We escorted them to the moon station and made the breathing announcement over the loudspeaker."

For the decor Smith covered the tables in silver Mylar, found rocks outside his own home and sprayed them blue, glittered them, and bought crimini mushrooms to build his centerpiece. He installed a black curtain on the wall behind 2,000 twinkle lights to make it appear to the seated guests at the tables that they were looking back at Earth. "That cost nothing to do," he says. "You could do it in your backyard. And a fog machine is only $50 to rent."

# The Menu

### Hors D'oeuvres
Grilled Shiitake Mushrooms with Sun-dried Tomato Relish
Cracked Pepper Beef Carpaccio with Roquefort Sauce
Stuffed Prawns with Fresh Spinach, Parmesan Cheese & Garlic
Blackened Sea Scallops on Braised Leeks with Cilantro Lime Sauce

### First Course
Belgian Endive with Yellow Pear Tomato
Tossed in a Balsamic Vinaigrette

### Entrée
Pan-roasted Sea Bass on Pearl Pasta with
Seasonal Vegetables & a
Yellow Pepper Sauce
or
Charred Fillet of Beef with a
Red Wine Demi Glaze

### Dessert
Chocolate Soufflé Pie
Fresh Fruit Plate
Fresh Brewed Coffee & Tea

# The Recipes

## Grilled Shiitake Mushrooms with Sun-dried Tomato Relish

### Crouton

Slice a baguette cross length approximately $1/4$ to $1/8$ inch. Sprinkle with olive oil and bake in the oven at 350° for three minutes or until golden brown. Let cool off to the side.

### Mushrooms

Select four medium (3-inch) firm cleaned shiitake mushrooms. Lightly toss with minced garlic, salt and pepper, and finely chopped fresh mixed herbs. Grill or sauté lightly or until liquor starts to bleed from the mushrooms, then let cool off to the side. Cut into thirds.

### Sun-dried Tomato Salsa

Rejuvenate sun-dried tomatoes in white wine by heating on the stove in a saucepan and bringing to a simmer. Set them aside for 5 to 10 minutes until soft, depending on the tomatoes. When the tomatoes have cooled, julienne and mix with olive oil, fresh minced garlic, and finely chopped fresh herbs. Add salt and pepper to taste.

TO SERVE: On the top of the crouton, place the cooled shiitake mushroom. Then sprinkle with the sun-dried tomato salsa and garnish with sprigs of fresh herbs.

## Tips

You're in control of the temper of the evening. A good party is like a good book. If it's boring, your guests will not finish it.

# Blackened Sea Scallops on Braised Leeks with Cilantro Lime Sauce

## Leeks

Clean and slice leeks to create rounds. In a sauté pan on medium heat, braise with olive oil, salt, and pepper. The leeks should cook slowly to sweat. This will allow them to soften and bring out their flavor. After 5 to 10 minutes, set aside.

## Scallops

Select fresh diver scallops or day boat scallops (u 12). Slice in half to make two equally tall, round scallop pieces. Roll in a mixture of Cajun spices (cumin, paprika, thyme, oregano, salt, pepper, chili powder, cayenne pepper, and garlic salt, or buy a Cajun seasoning to your liking). Sauté in a very hot pan with oil so that the scallops' crust blackens, but keep the scallops moist. The pan cannot be too hot. Quickly blacken both sides and set aside.

TO SERVE: While scallops are warm but not too hot, place the braised leek mixture on top of the scallops. Garnish with roasted corn kernels and diced roasted red peppers and serve.

## Stuffed Belgian Endive with Pear Tomatoes & Balsamic Vinaigrette

Select fresh Belgian endive that is slightly yellow in color and with no green tint (the green color is a sign that the endive has been around too long). Keep cool and in the dark until needed.

### Vinaigrette

Mix vigorously together two parts olive oil with one part aged balsamic vinegar. Season with salt and pepper to taste.

### Tomatoes

Slice red, yellow, and orange pear tomatoes in half and toss with slivered kalamata olives, toasted pine nuts, julienne roasted red peppers, julienne fresh basil, salt and pepper to taste.

TO SERVE: Toss tomato mixture with balsamic vinaigrette. Spoon the combined mixture on to the fresh endive leaves and serve.

## On Lighting

If you can't afford the spotlights, find two little lamps in your house and put nonflammable colored material over them to use as spotlights.

## Pan-roasted Sea Bass on Pearl Pasta with Seasonal Vegetables & Yellow Pepper Sauce
(SERVES 6)

6 sea bass fillets

1 Tbs. lemon juice

2 Tbs. olive oil

Salt and pepper to taste

Chopped fresh oregano, basil,

    and thyme

Sprinkle the sea bass with lemon juice and 1 Tbs. olive oil. Season with salt, pepper, and herbs. Heat remaining oil in large sauté pan, and cook 5 minutes (or more depending on thickness) on each side over medium heat.

### Yellow Pepper Sauce

1 Tbs. olive oil

1 medium onion, chopped

2 whole yellow peppers, diced

2 cups chicken stock

1/2 cup white wine

Heat oil over medium heat in a saucepan. Sauté onion and peppers until tender. Add white wine and simmer for 2 minutes, then add chicken stock and simmer for 15 minutes. Pass through food mill or sieve, and pour over fish or serve on the side.

*Blend is the word for everything…*

You've got to blend in the colors, the music, the food, the lighting. It all has to come together to make a whole concept.

**Pearl Pasta with Vegetables**

1 lb. pearl pasta

1 carrot, finely chopped

2 celery stalks, finely chopped

2 roma tomatoes, diced

1 cup thawed peas

1 small onion, finely chopped

2 Tbs. extra virgin olive oil

Salt and pepper to taste

6 large leaves fresh basil

1 cup freshly grated parmigiano reggiano

Sauté onion until tender, then add vegetables and cook until al dente. Boil pasta to desired doneness, drain, and toss with vegetables. Add remaining olive oil, add butter if desired, and toss with parmesan or serve on the side.

# Charred Fillet of Beef with a Red Wine Demi Glaze

## Red Wine Demi Glaze

5 lb. veal bones, roasted

1 celery stalk

3 large carrots

1 large onion

1 can tomato paste

1/2 cup red wine

3 shallots, chopped

Put veal bones, celery, carrots, and onion in 2 gallons water. Boil until reduced to 1 gallon. Add tomato paste, then reduce to 1/2 gallon. Add red wine and shallots, and boil another 15 minutes. Pour off red wine demi glaze.

## Charred Fillet of Beef

12 oz. best quality fillet of beef

1 Tbs. olive oil

Salt and pepper

Rub a mixture of olive oil, salt, and pepper quickly on each side and cook to desired doneness.

# Chocolate Soufflé Pie
(YIELD: 6 SOUFFLÉS)

Preparation time: 1 hour plus cooking time

INGREDIENTS

## Pie Crust

3 Tbs. unsalted butter, cut into pieces

1/4 cup granulated sugar

1 large egg yolk

1 1/2 tsp. heavy cream

3/4 cup all-purpose flour

## Soufflé Base

1/2 cup milk

1 vanilla bean, split in half lengthwise

1 1/2 Tbs. unsalted butter, chilled

1 1/2 Tbs. granulated sugar

1 1/2 Tbs. all-purpose flour

## Soufflé Batter

| | |
|---|---|
| 8 oz. semi-sweet chocolate | 1 Tbs. vanilla extract |
| 4 Tbs. unsalted butter, melted | 4 egg whites |
| 8 large egg yolks | 1 cup granulated sugar |
| 1 Tbs. brewed espresso | 1 tsp. cream of tartar |

*Need an idea for a 50th birthday party? Here's one from* **Thaddeus Smith:**

"How about a '50s sock hop? Do everything in pink and black and white. When your guests come in, give them a pair of socks to put on and let them wear socks around your house. They'll love it. You greet them at the door and say "Welcome to the '50s sock hop. Take your shoes off, here's a pair of socks." (The socks have the birthday boy or birthday girl's name and the number 50 on them). Just putting on those socks will automatically make everyone

## Garnish

Confectioners' sugar

Whipped cream

THE PIE CRUST: Position a rack in the oven and preheat to 350°. Lightly grease a 13"x 9 ½" baking pan. Line the bottom of the pan with parchment paper, and butter well. With a fork, vigorously mix the butter and sugar until thoroughly blended. Add the egg yolk, flour, and cream, mixing well until incorporated. The dough should be moist and hold together without crumbling or breaking apart.

On a well-floured work surface, gather the dough into a ball and divide into six equal pieces. By hand, shape 6 circles ¼ inch thick. Cut out to fit the ramekins. Place the 6 circles on the prepared pan. Lightly grease another sheet of parchment paper and place over the circles. Bake for 8 minutes until the circles are golden and the edges just begin to brown. Remove the baking pan from the oven and transfer the circles to a wire rack to cool. Increase the oven temperature to 375°.

MAKE THE SOUFFLÉ BASE: Pour the milk into a small saucepan. With a paring knife, scrape the inside of the vanilla bean into the milk. Bring the milk to a gentle boil.

Meanwhile, in a food processor fitted with a metal chopping blade, cream together the cold butter and the sugar. Add the flour, pulsing on and off until combined, about 15 seconds. When the milk has boiled, remove from the heat and strain through a metal sieve. Pour the milk back into the saucepan and, over medium-low heat, whisk in the butter mixture. Blend well until smooth. The mixture should thicken slightly. Set aside.

MAKE THE SOUFFLÉ BATTER: Melt the chocolate in a bowl over hot water. Melt the butter together with the chocolate. Remove from the heat and beat in the yolks, espresso, and vanilla. The mixture should be shiny and thick enough to coat the back of a spoon.

In the $4\frac{1}{2}$-quart bowl of a heavy-duty electric mixer, using the wire whip attachments, whip the egg whites until they form soft peaks. Slowly incorporate the sugar and cream of tartar. Beat until the egg whites are still and glossy.

Using a rubber spatula, fold the chocolate mixture into the egg whites, being careful not to deflate the egg whites. Fold the soufflé base into the egg mixture. Do not overmix.

On a $9\frac{1}{2}"$ x $13"$ baking sheet, place the circles inside the ramekins. Slowly pour the soufflé mixture, filling the ramekins. Place in the oven and bake for 20 minutes until puffed and lightly cracked.

Gently remove from the oven and allow the ramekins to cool on a wire rack. The soufflés will have risen over the tops of the ramekins. Dust the soufflés with confectioners' sugar and serve immediately in their ramekins with whipped cream.

there a part of what you are creating. Not only does it give them a gift, but it erases all inhibitions immediately.

# GAI KLASS

"DUSTIN HOFFMAN'S CHEF DESCRIBED IT BEST. He said, "Gai, your food is cozy." I love country and cozy and warm and welcoming, and I love a little fun in things. Life is too short to be serious all the time."

# The Affair

## Tony Puryear Wedding

What she loves—cozy, warm, welcoming, and fun, along with magnificent food—is only a fraction of what you get with event producer extraordinaire Gai Klass' special touch. Her parties—whether large affairs or smaller, more intimate ones—all have another thing in common: a stellar touch of class. But it is undoubtedly her unique sensibility, so obvious in the way she views her work, that sets Gai Klass apart.

"It's a very personal thing," she explains. "For me, every event is a labor of love, an extension of the way I care for people, the way I serve people, and the way I walk through life. But the most important thing to me is to capture the spirit of my clients in every way."

This enticing attitude appealed to screenwriter Tony Puryear. His marriage to actress Erica Alexander last summer was arranged in every detail by Klass. "She has an amazing bedside manner," says Puryear, whose most recent screenplay was for *Eraser*, starring Arnold Schwarzenegger. "She exudes competence and warmth. The food was spectacular. It looked absolutely beautiful. Everything was perfect."

Klass understood her clients well by the time she began designing the overall concept for the wedding, derived after hours of brainstorming with them. "They are very unique, bright, interesting people who have an open, embracing attitude about life," she explains. "There was a richness about their experiences and preferences that I wanted to reflect. They wanted the wedding to be unique, personal, a little offbeat, anything goes. It had to be truly personalized and in very good taste."

According to Puryear, that is precisely what it was. "It's like putting a diamond in a good setting," he explains. "That's what Gai did for us by arranging the whole thing, even down to the invitations. They were stunning, rimmed in gold, and they set the tone for this rich, exotic, funky look we had."

It began with a perfect setting: a majestic stone manor on a romantic bluff in Malibu. Guests were serenaded by a classical string quartet when they arrived. Cocktails—including frosty mint juleps appropriate for the heat of the late September day—were served on the terrace, with a spectacular sunset as the backdrop. The pre-ceremony hors d'oeuvres reflected the diversity of the cuisine that was in store: fresh figs with prosciutto and lime juice; smoked salmon; celery root, corn, and potato pancakes; and crispy tortillas filled with avocado and crab. The ceremony itself was traditional, but the mood changed the instant the couple kissed, as flamboyant flamenco guitarists began playing and led the guests to a bluff overlooking the ocean where more cocktails and hors d'oeuvres were served.

For dinner, the guests moved to an area bathed in red, orange, and gold lights that enhanced the tables, lined in black undercloths and silky metallic overlays in exotic shades of green, red, and gold. Lavishly strewn over the middle of each table, among multitudes of oversized candles, were lush marigolds in deep golds, rich reds, and oranges. Puryear loved what he saw. "It was very sexy," he says. "Flowers dripping off of everything. The colors were dark, sexy, and warm, very exotic looking." An Indian ensemble played from a pillow-lined platform. The tables were set with glass chargers rimmed with gold beads. In keeping with her innovative flair, Klass used oversized martini glasses for the first course, a Shrimp Cocktail served with Bloody Mary sorbet and emerald juice with a splash of vermouth.

And then came the entrée—crispy roast duck with acacia honey and cider vinegar sauce. The cake, a traditional white cake with hazelnut frosting, was a work of art. Designed to reflect the gown of the bride, it appeared to be made of lace and was decorated with brightly colored flowers.

After dinner, the party progressed to a two-story disco. The lounge downstairs was filled with plush cushions where people could relax and enjoy cappuccinos when they were not dancing upstairs to the music of the wild and hot Pink Martinis, the band selected by the bride and groom.

It was, by all accounts, a grand affair, well represented by a celebrity crowd the groom refers to as "very-hard-to-impress Hollywood folks who think they've seen it all. And still," he says, "I know my guests had never seen food or a wedding like this before. So many people walked away saying, 'Wow. When I get married, that's the way I want it done.'"

# The Menu

## Tray-passed Hors D'oeuvres

All hors d'oeuvres are passed by our uniformed wait staff
on beautiful trays that reflect and complement the color,
texture, or ethnic flavor of the dish selected

### Before the Ceremony

Fresh Figs with Prosciutto
and Lime Juice

Smoked Salmon Rose
Celery Root, Corn & Potato Pancakes
Crème Fraîche
American #1 Sturgeon Caviar

Crispy Tortillas Filled with Avocado & Crab
Salsa Cruda

**Dessert**

# Old-fashioned Apple Crisp with Apple Cider Caramel Ice Cream

# Sorbets

Served with a splash of champagne
in a champagne glass with a cluster of champagne grapes

Raspberry

Lemon

Green Apple

# Homemade Cookies

Shortbread Heart

Raspberry Linzer Hearts

Chocolate Hearts

# French Roast & Decaffeinated French Roast-Colombian Blend Coffees
# Assorted Teas

# The Recipes

## Shrimp Cocktail with Bloody Mary Sorbet & Emerald Juice
Inspired by Hans Rockenwagner

6 ribs of celery, with leaves
   attached

1 1/2 cups tomato sorbet, made
   with 2 dashes Tabasco sauce

9 Tbs. Hansen's mixed greens juice

Dash of vermouth

18 extra-large cooked shrimp,
   with tail shells

1/2 small bunch chives, cut into
   1 1/2-inch lengths, for garnish

6 martini glasses

### Bloody Mary Sorbet
(YIELD: 3 1/2 CUPS)

6 vine-ripened plum tomatoes,
   peeled and seeded

1/2 cup sugar syrup (1/2 cup water
   and 1/3 cup sugar; stir until sugar
   is dissolved; boil one minute)

1 Tbs. freshly squeezed lemon juice

1 1/2 tsp. tomato paste

1/2 tsp. salt

1/4 tsp. freshly ground white pepper

1 tsp. finely chopped chives

4 Tbs. Stolichnaya or Ketel One
   vodka

In a blender or food processor, combine the tomatoes, sugar syrup, lemon juice, tomato paste, salt, white pepper, and vodka. Process until completely smooth, scraping down the sides of the bowl as necessary. Adjust seasonings and stir in the chives. Freeze in an ice cream maker until mixture has reached desired consistency.

## Tips

ALTERNATE METHOD: Instead of using an ice cream maker, transfer to a large stainless steel bowl, taste for seasoning, and stir in the chives. Place the bowl, uncovered, in the freezer. About every 15 minutes for 2 hours, remove the bowl from the freezer and whisk the sorbet. If ice crystals form, return the mixture to the blender or food processor and blend again. Cover and store in the freezer until ready to serve.

TO ASSEMBLE: Trim the bottoms of the celery ribs so that they will extend 4 inches above the rim of the glass. Divide the sorbet among the 6 martini glasses. Place 1 celery rib upright in the sorbet in each glass. Drizzle 1½ Tbs. of the mixed greens juice, as well as a splash of vermouth, around the edge of each glass. Hang 3 shrimp, tail ends outward, over the rim of each glass. Garnish with several lengths of chive. Serve immediately.

## Avocado Blini

Inspired by Pawleys Island Inn in South Carolina
(YIELD: 24–30 MINI BLINIS)

2 eggs, lightly beaten

²/₃ cup flour

¹/₂ tsp. salt

¹/₄ cup whole milk

Pulp of 1 ripe avocado (about 5 oz.), pureed in a blender or food
    processor (or mashed by hand until no lumps remain)

1–3 Tbs. butter, melted

A little lemon juice (in the batter)

Fresh ground pepper, to taste

Combine the eggs, flour, salt, milk, avocado, and lemon juice.
Add pepper to taste. Stir until the batter is well blended. The
mixture will be fairly thick, like cornbread batter.

Lightly butter and then heat a griddle or skillet. For each blini,
use 1 tablespoon of batter and spread it out on the griddle into a
circle about 1 ¹/₂ inches in diameter. Cook over medium-low heat
for about 1 minute on each side, until golden brown. The blini
will still be moist within, rather like guacamole with a crust.
Repeat until you have cooked all the batter.

## Squash Blossoms with Italian Fontina, Deep-fried

Inspired by Alice Waters
(SERVES 6)

| | |
|---|---|
| ¼ cup Italian parsley leaves | 2 eggs |
| 4 or 5 cloves garlic | ¼ cup milk |
| 20 fresh open squash blossoms | 1 cup fine cornmeal |
| ½ pound tasty Italian fontina cheese, grated | About ½ cup black olives |

Mince ¼ cup Italian parsley together with 4–5 cloves garlic, and mix with cheese. Open up the individual blossoms wide enough to insert cheese mixture. Fill each blossom, then twist the ends of the blossoms together gently. Beat 2 eggs together with ¼ cup milk. Dip each blossom into the egg-milk mixture and then roll quickly and evenly in the cornmeal. Refrigerate for a minimum of 10 minutes. Deep-fry the blossoms in canola oil at 350° to 400° for about 2-3 minutes, or until they begin to brown and the cheese is melted. Drain on paper towels and serve immediately, garnished with lots of Italian parsley or fresh basil sprigs and black olives.

## Chinese Cinnamon-Plum Dip

Inspired by Hugh Carpenter
(YIELD: APPROX. ¾ CUP)

| | |
|---|---|
| 9 Tbs. plum sauce | 1 Tbs. lemon juice |
| 2¼ Tbs. dry sherry | ½ tsp. ground cinnamon |

Combine ingredients for dip, and stir well.

# Vietnamese Vegetable Spring Rolls

Inspired by Sharon Fagen
(YIELD: 24 SMALL INDIVIDUAL SPRING ROLLS)

## Filling

| | |
|---|---|
| 1 oz. dried Chinese bean threads | 2 Tbs. julienne carrots (peel first) |
| 2 Tbs. julienne scallions (use green part only) | 2 Tbs. slivered bamboo shoots |
| 2 Tbs. slivered water chestnuts | 1 Tbs. each of finely chopped fresh mint and finely chopped |
| 2 Tbs. canned straw mushrooms, drained | fresh chervil |

## Dressing

| | |
|---|---|
| 1 Tbs. rice wine vinegar (use light kind only) | 1/8 tsp. ground ginger |
| 1/2 Tbs. vegetable oil | 1/2 tsp. sugar |
| 1/2 Tbs. sesame oil | Pinch of salt and pepper |

## Rolls

6–8 large Vietnamese rice paper rounds

6 lettuce leaves, torn into quarters

Place the bean threads in boiling water and cook for 4 minutes, then drain well and place on paper towel to absorb extra water. Combine the bean threads in a small bowl with the carrots, scallions, bamboo shoots, water chestnuts, mushrooms, mint, and chervil. Set aside. Combine the rice vinegar, sesame oil, vegetable oil, and ginger in a

*Tips*

Try not to do crowded plates.

They shouldn't be sparse either. I

like people to feel that they're

well taken care of and well fed. A

plate burgeoned with food is

unappealing and off-putting. But

people never go home hungry

from my parties.

small bowl. Mix well. Add sugar and mix. Add a pinch of salt and pepper and mix well. Taste and adjust seasonings if necessary. Pour dressing over the filling ingredients and combine until well mixed. Set aside.

TO ASSEMBLE: Find a tray or bowl large enough to hold the rice rounds and fill with a bit of water. Dip the rice round into the water until both sides are wet. Fold rice round in half. Working the long way, take a 2" x 4" piece of lettuce and place at the bottom of the round. Put 1 tablespoon of the filling mixture inside the leaf. Roll tightly, rolling until you reach the top of the round. Trim the edges of the roll so they are even, then cut each roll into four identical pieces. Store covered with damp paper towel until service.

## Sesame Soy Sauce
(YIELD: ½ CUP)

4 Tbs. light soy sauce

2 Tbs. Chinese sesame oil

2 Tbs. red wine vinegar

1 scallion, sliced crosswise
  into tiny rings

1 clove garlic, minced

Crushed red pepper, to taste

Combine first 5 ingredients. Add crushed pepper to taste. Store airtight in refrigerator until needed.

## Corn Cakes
(YIELD: 17 REGULAR-SIZE MUFFINS)

2 sticks butter

1/4 cup sugar

4 eggs

1 4-oz. can diced chili peppers
  (Ortega brand)

1 cup creamed corn

1/2 cup each grated jack and
  cheddar cheese

1/2 tsp. salt

1 cup flour

1 cup yellow cornmeal

4 tsp. baking powder

Preheat oven to 350°. Grease muffin tins. Cream butter and sugar until light and fluffy. Add eggs, one at a time, then peppers, corn, and cheeses, beating well after each addition. Add dry ingredients and combine. Mix only until moistened (do not overmix). Fill muffin tins to 2/3 full. Bake 35–45 minutes, until toothpick inserted in center comes out with a few moist crumbs clinging to it.

## Stoneground Wheat & Molasses Bread
Inspired by Dory Ford
(YIELD: 1 LARGE LOAF OR 2 SMALL)

2 tsp. active dry yeast

11 oz. all-purpose flour

1 3/4 oz. rye flour

5 3/4 oz. whole wheat flour

3/4 oz. wheat germ

1 3/4 tsp. salt

1 Tbs. sugar

Mix above ingredients.

11 1/2 oz. hot water

1/3 cup molasses

1/2 oz. cornflakes

3 Tbs. butter (melted)

Combine and mix dry ingredients. Add water, molasses, and melted butter. Mix in an electric mixer with a dough hook on low for 10 minutes, or knead by hand for 10 minutes. Shape into loaf, 2 loaves, or rolls. Cover with a tea towel and place in a warm, dry place to rise until doubled in size. Bake in a preheated oven at 375° until done (45 minutes to 1 hour for loaves; 25–30 minutes for rolls).

## Roast Duck in Acacia Honey & Cider Vinegar Sauce

Inspired by Perla Meyers

1 tsp. whole coriander seeds

2 ducks, 4–4 1/2 lbs. each

1 Tbs. tomato paste

Salt and freshly ground

2 Tbs. light soy sauce

   white pepper

2 Tbs. cider vinegar

3 Tbs. unsalted butter

1 1/2 tsp. orange honey

2 tsp. dried thyme

3/4 cup chicken stock

4 Tbs. unsalted butter

1/2 tsp. ground coriander

1 tsp. canola oil

1 Tbs. each softened butter &

1 1/2 cup chicken stock

   flour, mixed into a paste

2 large shallots, peeled and

   (beurre manié)

   finely minced

Several hours in advance of roasting duck, or the day before if possible, prepare the honey-soy mixture. In a small skillet, toast the coriander seeds until fragrant. Crush in a mortar and pestle and combine with the soy sauce, honey, and ground coriander in a small bowl. Blend well and set aside.

## Tips

I have always told clients — and it

truly works — to choose foods

they adore for the menu. If it's a

sit-down dinner and you love

goose or lamb, use it. You do not

have to always be safe or select

foods you think everyone will eat.

Select the foods you love the

most. In my experience those are

the most successful parties, and

the ones for which we always get

the greatest number of raves

about the food.

Preheat oven to 350°. Dry the ducks thoroughly with paper towels. Season with salt, white pepper, and thyme, and truss the ducks. Heat ½ of the butter and the oil in a large baking dish. Add the ducks and brown on all sides. Add the chicken stock and roast the ducks in the center of the oven for 2 hours and 45 minutes, basting every 15 minutes with the stock and removing some of the fat at the same time. When the ducks are done, remove to a baking sheet and set aside. Halve the ducks carefully, keeping skin equal and intact. Remove the breast and thigh bone. Strain the pan juices into a bowl and thoroughly degrease. Set the juices aside.

Add the remaining butter to the pan and melt over medium heat. Add the shallots, and sauté until soft and lightly browned. Add the tomato paste and cider vinegar, bring to a boil, and cook until the vinegar has almost evaporated. Add the honey and soy mixture, bring to a boil, and add the ¾ cup chicken stock and reserved pan juices. Lower the heat and simmer the sauce until somewhat reduced, tasting it to ensure it does not become too salty.

Remove from heat and whisk in beurre manié and cook until sauce lightly coats the back of a spoon. Taste and correct the seasoning. Strain the sauce into a saucepan and whisk in the extra 3 Tbs. of butter for enrichment. Keep sauce warm, but do not boil. Preheat broiler. Place the boned duck halves under the broiler, 6—8 inches from the source of heat, and broil until the skin is nicely browned and crisp. Transfer the ducks to a cutting board. Carve and serve with the sauce.

# Pearl Barley Risotto
Inspired by Dory Ford

| | |
|---|---|
| 1 shallot, minced | 4 Tbs. additional butter |
| 2 Tbs. butter | 4 cups chicken stock |
| 1 cup mixed chopped herbs such as basil, parsley, mint, and chervil | 1 cup chicken stock reduction (see note) |
| 2 cups pearl barley, rinsed | 1 additional cup of chicken or |
| 2 Tbs. finely diced, raw carrots | duck stock |

Sauté shallots in butter. Add barley and stir to coat. Add stock and simmer on low, in a covered pot, until stock is absorbed. If barley is still hard after adding 4 cups of stock, add a little more stock. Cook until al dente but not gluey. Then mix in 2 Tbs. finely minced carrot. The risotto can be made 1 day in advance and stored, covered, in the refrigerator.

TO FINISH: Heat large Teflon pan and add 4 Tbs. butter. When the butter is melted, add 1 cup mixed chopped herbs and sauté briefly, being careful not to brown the herbs. Add broken-up risotto. Stir until heated through, then add 1 cup chicken stock reduction plus an additional cup of duck or chicken stock. Season with salt and pepper, to taste. Simmer uncovered, stirring frequently, until the consistency is thick and creamy. Spoon out onto plates or mold into timbales.

NOTE: To make 1 cup of chicken stock reduction, boil 2 cups of stock over high heat until reduced by half.

## Tips

Be in the moment with your guests. Be flexible and willing to change your plan. If you've put the tray of stationary hors d'oeuvres in one room and your guests have gathered in another, don't be afraid to move the tray.

# Old-fashioned Apple Crisp with Apple Cider Caramel Ice Cream

## Caramel Sauce
(MAKES APPROXIMATELY 3 CUPS)

| | |
|---|---|
| 1 pound granulated sugar | 1/2 tsp. lemon juice |
| 1/3 cup water | 2 Tbs. light corn syrup |
| 1 1/2 cups heavy cream | 2 oz. unsalted butter |

Place the sugar, water and lemon juice in a small saucepan. Bring to a boil. Brush down the sides of the pan with a clean brush dipped in water. Add the corn syrup. Cook over medium heat until the syrup reaches a golden amber color.

Remove the pan from the heat and add the heavy cream carefully. Stand back as you pour in the cream as the mixture may splatter. Stir to mix in the cream. If the sauce is not smooth, return the pan to the heat and cook, stirring constantly, to melt any lumps.

Add the butter (with the pan off the heat). Keep stirring until the butter has melted and the sauce is smooth.

## Apple Crisp Topping
(x1 = 6 cups, x2 = 12 cups)

| | |
|---|---|
| 1 1/2 cups quick-cooking oatmeal (not instant) | 1 1/2 cups dark brown sugar |
| | 1/2 cup flour |
| 1/2 cup whole wheat flour | 2 tsp. cinnamon |
| 3/4 cup chopped pecans or walnuts | 1 cup (2 sticks) butter, softened |

Bake in preheated, hot oven (425° F) for about 35 minutes.

## Tips

If I have a single piece of advice,

it's organize, organize, organize.

The more time and effort put into

organizing in advance, the more

relaxed and smooth-flowing the

event will be. When you want the

event to look really spontaneous,

you have to really work ahead of

time. The amount of work you do

ahead of time is conversely pro-

portionate to how spontaneous it

appears to be.

## Lacy Ice Cream Shells

1/4 cup finely ground blanched almonds

3/4 cup sweet butter,
   room temperature

3/4 cup sugar

4 tsp. flour

2 Tbs. milk

Melted chocolate to coat

Combine first five ingredients into a smooth paste. Cut parchment into 6-inch squares on each baking sheet. Place 1 large Tbs. of dough in the center of each square. Flatten with wet fingers until about 1/2-inch thick. Bake at 350° for 12–13 minutes. Let set 1 minute. Place upside down on 3-inch Pyrex or glass bowls. Remove paper very quickly. Brush insides with chocolate, which will be delicious and protect the shell when filled.

## Apple Cider Ice Cream
(MAKES ABOUT 1½ QUARTS)

8 egg yolks

2 cups milk

2 large cinnamon sticks

2 cups heavy cream

1½ cups dry sparkling
   apple cider

Whisk the egg yolks lightly in a large bowl and set aside. Scald the cream and milk in a large, heavy saucepan and keep warm over low heat.

Combine the apple cider, sugar, and cinnamon sticks in a noncorrodible saucepan. Cook over high heat until the mixture reduces and turns a dark amber color, 20 to 25 minutes. Remove the cinnamon sticks and immediately begin whisking the mixture into the warm cream and milk, incorporating about a third at a time. (Be careful; the cream will spatter and bubble up. But the caramelized cider must be poured into the cream as quickly as possible or it will continue to cook and burn in the pan.) When all the caramel has been whisked in, reheat the cream, stirring constantly, until the cider is completely incorporated.

Pour a quarter of the hot mixture into the egg yolks, whisking continuously, then pour it back into the saucepan over low heat, stirring constantly with a wooden spoon until the mixture thickens enough to coat the back of the spoon. Strain the custard through a fine mesh strainer into a bowl. Whisk it a few times to release the heat, then refrigerate until thoroughly chilled. Freeze the custard in an ice cream freezer.

Dinner in the presence of

His Royal Highness
The Prince of Wales


Menu

Roasted Pumpkin filled with shrimp, scallops and lobster
(in a champagne sauce)

Roast Poussin with Wild Mushrooms
Potato Fondant
Gateau of Roasted Vegetables

White Chocolate Swan with Ice Creams

Coffee
Chocolate Truffles

Simi 1992 Chardonnay
Simi 1990 Cabernet Sauvignon

# LA CUISINE

*Tom Byrne*

"YOU MUST ADAPT CONSTANTLY. There's no hard line because things change. The location, the weather, the number of people, the physical site—everything that can change, does."

# The Affair

## Dinner in the Presence of His Royal Highness, the Prince of Wales

It was truly an affair fit for a king, which was a good thing. The guest of honor was His Royal Highness, the Prince of Wales. Prince Charles, who has long taken an interest in the problems of the inner city, had been invited by the mayor of Los Angeles to see the regeneration of the city after the riots that had taken place there 18 months earlier. In support of the Prince's visit, a Celebration of British Arts Festival had been planned to benefit local charities and the British arts. A gala sit-down dinner for 220, at the home of producer Aaron Spelling and his wife, Candy, was to be the crowning event of the weeklong occasion.

The Spellings are arguably as discriminating when it comes to the entertaining they do within the walls of their mansion, known to insiders as "The Manor," as any member of royalty would be, and they had no question about the caterer they wanted for the prince's banquet. There was but one man they trusted enough, one of the few who had done events of this stature many times in the past. He was a caterer of exceptional ability, quality, taste, and class who was also a masterful chef. He had catered events in the highest echelons of Washington, D.C., doing countless dinners for the State Department and other lofty political agencies. He had worked in New York with Glorious Foods, the finest of the Big Apple's finest caterers. He had himself been a chef at one of that city's foremost restaurants. And he had finally come to Los Angeles in 1989 to start his own catering business, using every iota of the knowledge and experience he had gleaned over the years to maximize his unparalleled talent. His name was Tom Byrne, and the name of his company was La Cuisine.

One need only examine the menu for this particular event to understand the matchless quality Byrne brings to all the affairs he creates, which run the gamut from Hollywood movie premiere parties to private dinners across the country—and around the world—for celebrities in every walk of life. For His Royal Highness, there were but a few simple stipulations for the cuisine of the evening. Among the prince's "likes" were cream, chicken, foul, veal, and cream pudding desserts. Among his dislikes: red meat. After weeks of planning, testing, and tasting, the carte du jour was finalized. The first course would be hot: a roasted pumpkin filled with shrimp, scallops, and lobster in a champagne sauce. The main course would be a poussin, or baby chicken, with wild mushrooms, to be served with a potato fondant and a gâteau of roasted vegetables. Dessert would be a work of art in its own right: 220 individually sculpted white chocolate swans, crafted by world-renowned chocolatier Joseph Schmidt and flown in from San Francisco for the event. So delicate were the miniature swans that each was shipped in two separate pieces to prevent the fragile necks from breaking, to be artfully reassembled later by Byrne after their safe arrival in Los Angeles.

For La Cuisine there were, however, important considerations aside from the food, such as the logistics required to assure that the timing of the event was perfect: that the hot food would be served piping hot and the cold food would be served cold. This required a seamless strategy. The site of the dining room was an outdoor tent more than 100 yards from the Spellings' professionally equipped kitchen, where the food was to be prepared, so a "satellite kitchen" was created just outside the tent. Immediately prior to serving, each course would be taken there, covered. It would then be uncovered, sauced, and carried into the tent.

Still, as Tom Byrne knew only too well, at any affair one must be prepared for the unpredictable, and the royal dinner was to be no exception. It gave credence to the maxim that has become a staple in Byrne's professional life: the need to be flexible and to adapt. As it happened, the weather that evening was unseasonably cold. Cocktails, which were originally to be served outdoors around the pool, had to be moved indoors. This entailed only a minor adjustment, and it gave the guests a welcome opportunity to see the inside of The Manor. But the more difficult challenge came when it was learned, after all the guests had arrived, that the prince's arrival would be delayed by at least an hour. Not a course could be prepared in advance so Byrne made his calculations accordingly. "Once Prince

Charles arrived we knew we had another 30 minutes," he explains, "and that's when we started cooking."

Byrne and his 15-member kitchen staff worked with masterful precision. By the time the guests had made their way down the 100-foot runner that led from the front door to the tent, the rest of the La Cuisine staff—3 captains and 30 white-coated, white-gloved waiters—were ready to begin waiting tables. The guests were seated at 22 tables in the 60' x 90' tent. It had taken six full days to install the structure, but the effort was clearly worth it. The carpeted dining room was stunning. Colors of peach, white, and gold warmed the large chamber and seemed to cast their own glow upon the tables, which were covered with ivory tablecloths and gold overlays. The plates were white with gold rims. Centered among the cut crystal glassware and flickering candelabras were sumptuous bouquets of gorgeous white tulips.

The food was predictably extraordinary, but perhaps the most impressive point of the dinner was the flawless presentation of dessert. The swans had been filled with ice cream, which could not be allowed to melt. To guarantee this, the 220 desserts were carefully arranged upon a table eight feet in length. Then the entire table, replete with swans, was lifted up by Byrne and his staff and carried—ever so carefully—the hundred yards to the entrance of the tent. The ice cream stayed cold without mishap. And thus concluded a flawless meal.

The dinner's program included a brief speech by His Royal Highness, who was introduced by actress Angela Lansbury. When the fairy-tale evening ended and everyone had left content, one simple fact remained: The Spellings had been right. Tom Byrne was the perfect man for the job.

# The Menu

### First Course
Roasted Pumpkins Filled with
Shrimp, Scallops & Lobster in a Champagne Sauce
Herb-buttered Toast

### Entrée
Roasted Poussin with Wild Mushrooms
Gâteau of Roasted Vegetables
Potato Fondant

### Dessert
White Chocolate Swan
Surrounded by Assorted Sorbet & Fresh Fruit
Chocolate Truffles
Coffee

Simi 1990 Cabernet Sauvignon
Simi 1992 Chardonnay

# The Recipes

## Roasted Pumpkins Filled with Shrimp, Scallops & Lobster in a Champagne Sauce

Inspired by Jean-Claude Nedelec, friend & mentor of Tom Byrne
(YIELD: 6 SERVINGS)

### Pumpkins

Select 6 miniature pumpkins (orange, yellow, or white) at least 2 inches tall. Carefully cut 2-inch round openings in tops. Clean interiors of all seeds and fibers. Season interiors with salt and black pepper. Lightly oil skins and tops. Roast for 15-30 minutes at 350° until pumpkins have a burnished, slightly brown color. Reserve.

### Court Bouillon

| | |
|---|---|
| 1 gallon cold water | 2 celery stalks, chopped coarse |
| 1 cup white wine | 2 bay leaves |
| 2 carrots, chopped coarse | 1 Tbs. dry thyme |
| 1 leek, chopped coarse and rinsed | 1 Tbs. black peppercorn |
| | 1 Tbs. salt |

Bring to boil; reduce heat; simmer 20 minutes.

## Seafood

1 2-lb. lobster

18 large shrimp (shell on)

12 large sea scallops

Using a basket strainer, lower sea scallops into simmering court bouillon. Allow to poach 4 minutes. Remove; reserve. Repeat with shrimp. Simmer 4 minutes. Strain; reserve. Add lobster. Cook 12 minutes. While lobster cooks, shell and devein shrimp. Remove tail. When lobster has cooled, remove tail and claw meat. Remove cartilage from claws and halve. Slice tail into 12 medallions. Reserve.

## Sauce

| | |
|---|---|
| 3 cups court bouillon | 3 Tbs. all-purpose flour |
| 1 cup brut champagne | 1 cup heavy cream |
| 3 Tbs. shallots | Salt and white pepper |
| 3 Tbs. butter | |

Strain 3 cups court bouillon into a medium saucepan and reduce over medium heat to 1½ cups. Add one cup brut champagne and reduce by half again. Sauté 3 Tbs. shallots in 3 Tbs. butter over medium heat. When shallots are transparent, stir in 3 Tbs. all-purpose flour. Combine. Gradually whisk in champagne reduction. Whisk until smooth. Add 1 cup heavy cream. Bring to boil. Reduce heat, simmer 5 minutes. Add salt and white pepper to taste. Remove from heat until ready to assemble.

TO ASSEMBLE: Place pumpkin on baking pan 20 minutes before serving. Divide seafood among the six pumpkins. Cover pan with foil and heat through, 10–15 minutes in 350° oven. Heat sauce. Remove pumpkin from oven. Top with hot sauce. Garnish with chopped chives. Transfer to plates. Serve immediately.

NOTE: You may substitute halved acorn squash for pumpkins.

## Roasted Poussin with Wild Mushrooms

Preheat oven to 400°. Rinse and thoroughly pat dry (inside and out) 6 fresh poussin. Lightly season with salt, black pepper, and chopped fresh rosemary. Truss with kitchen twine. Arrange on baking pan and roast uncovered for 15 minutes. Reduce heat to 325° and continue to roast for additional 30 minutes or until juice runs clear when thigh is pricked. Remove from oven and cool enough to handle; with a small sharp knife carefully remove both breasts. Remove legs. Separate drumstick from thigh. Remove thigh bone. On clean baking pan place both pieces of boned thigh meat beside each other. Place breast on top of thigh meat. Repeat for remaining birds. (Drumsticks are not used in this recipe.)

## Mushroom Sauce

| | |
|---|---|
| 1/2 lb. medium shiitake mush-rooms, stemmed | 4 Tbs. olive oil |
| | I Tbs. butter |
| 1/2 lb. cremini mushrooms, quartered | I Tbs. chopped fresh thyme |
| | I Tbs. chopped fresh rosemary |
| I cup dry morels, soaked, stemmed, rinsed, drained | 2 Tbs. arrowroot |
| | 1/2 cup cold water |
| 1/4 cup finely diced shallots | 3 cups chicken stock |

Heat oil over medium-high heat in sauté pan. Add shiitake and cremini mushrooms. Sauté, stirring occasionally for 5 minutes. Add morels, shallots, rosemary, thyme, and butter. Sauté additional 5 minutes, stirring occasionally. Add chicken stock. Simmer uncovered for about 8 minutes. Add $1/2$ tsp. salt and $1/2$ tsp. ground white pepper. Mix arrowroot with cold water. Stir into simmering sauce. Adjust seasoning. Simmer an additional 5 minutes.

TO SERVE: Place baking pan with birds in 300° oven for 12–15 minutes to heat through. Transfer to plates or serving platter. Ladle small amount of sauce on top. Pass additional sauce separately.

# Gâteau of Roasted Vegetables
(SERVES 6)

12 ½-inch slices of medium-sized eggplant, lightly salted

12 ¼-inch slices yellow or red tomato

3 whole roasted red peppers (see note)

18 bias-cut slices of yellow squash

1 onion, diced medium

1 clove garlic, peeled and smashed

2 Tbs. olive oil

1 tsp. dry thyme

1 tsp. black pepper

11 tsp. salt

Peel and remove seeds from roasted pepper. Open and lay flat on cutting board, skin side down. With 3-inch cookie cutter or sharp knife, cut 2 circles from each pepper. Having sliced eggplant, chop any scraps into cubes. Sauté onion, garlic, and remaining scraps of pepper and eggplant in olive oil. Add dry thyme, black pepper, and salt. Stir occasionally to avoid sticking. When onions are transparent, transfer mixture to food processor. Flash to make thick paste. Scrape down bowl to ensure even consistency. Adjust seasoning. Lightly season sliced tomatoes, eggplant, and yellow zucchini. Grill lightly on both sides. Assemble gâteau starting with eggplant, then sliced tomato, roasted peppers, eggplant, tomato, and finally sliced zucchini (see photo), using a bit of paste as "glue" between layers. Transfer to lightly oiled baking pan.

TO SERVE: Bake for 10–15 minutes at 350° until piping hot. Carefully transfer to plates or platters with spatula.

NOTE: To roast peppers, place under broiler, over gas flame, on heated griddle surface, or on outdoor grill. Turn peppers as each side blackens. When charred and blistered on all sides, transfer to medium-size mixing bowl and cover with Saran Wrap (this will steam the peppers and the skins will come off more easily).

## Potato Fondant
(SERVES 6)

Using a sharp, small knife, pare baking potato into 1½-inch-thick slices. (Depending on size, yield will be 2 or 3 slices per potato.) Place 12 slices into lightly oiled, heavy-bottomed sauté pan or sauce pot. (Potatoes should fit snugly in cooking vessel.)

Place pan over medium heat. Add ¼ lb. (1 stick) butter to pan. Cover potatoes loosely with foil so steam escapes but heat is retained. Cook 20 minutes. Carefully turn potatoes and cook an additional 15 minutes, loosely covered.

Check for doneness by piercing with sharp knife. Knife should penetrate potatoes easily. Season with salt and white pepper.

NOTE: May be prepared in advance, but not refrigerated. To reheat, transfer to baking pan and warm in 350° oven 5 minutes.

Tom Byrne and partner Robyn Leuthe

# Market Catering & Event Planning

*Lili Goldstein McLean,
Robin Goldstein & Jeff McLean*

"OUR BUSINESS REVOLVES AROUND OUR PASSIONS: COOKING AND ENTERTAINING. Passion is the force behind everything we do. We believe food should be creative, party planning inventive."

# The Affair

## The Wedding of Television Executive
## Michael King

Their passion for what they do is distinctly apparent in every event that bears their divine touch. Take that passion and combine it with the innovative, exquisite food of two highly skilled chefs; add an extraordinary versatility in cuisines and ingenious presentations; finish it off with an endless stream of personal caring, and you will have the winning recipe for the hottest new catering company in town.

Lili and Jeff McLean and Lili's sister, Robin Goldstein, are the forceful trio behind Market Catering. They have proved that there is strength in numbers—especially when those numbers include two sisters who grew up learning every aspect of their family-owned restaurant business in Maryland and a guy who is, like Robin, an accomplished chef. With the newly configured family business, the formula remains unbeatable. Lili oversees the details of event planning—conceptualization with clients and organization—and has a natural ability to provide that rare personal touch.

The rewarding blend of these complementary talents was never more evident than at the wedding Market Catering did recently in Brentwood, California, for television producer and distributor (*Inside Edition, Oprah, Hard Copy*) Michael King and Jena, his new bride. Jeff, Lili, and Robin were already well known to the Kings, having catered several events for them, including an authentic Moroccan banquet for 80 at their home. But for their wedding, the Kings wanted a genuine Italian villa theme, and they'd assumed the best way to get it was to have it catered by an Italian restaurant. They were even prepared, if necessary, to fly staff in from an Italian restaurant in New York. But after a coast-to-coast search for the best way to create what they wanted, they found what they were looking for in their own backyard. Robin Goldstein had studied in Italy, and Jeff was proficient in a multitude of ethnic cuisines, with Italian foremost on his list. Jena, who had already spent considerable time sampling the best restaurants in the country, was duly impressed. "I started doing Market's tastings," she says. "Not only is their food the best, but they're also so calm and well organized."

The deal was done. Market brought in designer Douglas Johnson to make everything else—linens, music, flowers, decor—as authentically Italian as the food. When they were done they had created precisely what the Kings had dreamed of: a veritable Italian villa.

The first thing guests saw as they came up the driveway was a bouquet of hundreds of orange and yellow roses fashioned into a pineapple, a symbol of welcome. At the front of the house, two large lion medallions, reminiscent of the gold lions that had adorned the wedding invitations, guarded each side of the door. In the front courtyard, an Italian trio played festive accordion music beside a bubbling fountain, covered with lush, opulent flowers brought in for the occasion. Champagne was handed to arriving guests, who could enjoy the serenade as they sat at the canopied wooden Italian tables.

That was only the beginning. Guests were asked to move through the house to the backyard, where the mood changed from lighthearted and festive to romantic and tranquil. Two more French lions, this time wreathed in red roses, greeted guests, and the fanciful serenade was replaced by ethereal Irish Riverdance music, played by a band put together by singer Lionel Richie's band director. Guests—including actress Roseanne, boxer Sugar Ray Leonard and wife Bernadette, and attorney Robert Shapiro—sat in rows of Italian wood chairs with burgundy cushions for the ceremony. Barbra Streisand and her fiancé, Jim Brolin, joined the guests on the perimeter of the area, which comprised commodious, overstuffed white couches. The aisle was lined with opulent swags of roses in jewel colors, and the canopy under which the couple would stand was thickly covered with delicate rose petals.

Before guests were seated for dinner, there was a delicious post-ceremony interlude of cocktails and hors d'oeuvres: Tuscan pizza, chargrilled shrimp skewers, grilled eggplant rolled with a goat cheese filling, carpaccio of beef tenderloin served on crostini, and bruschetta with red and yellow tomatoes. For the dinner, guests entered a breathtaking structure that had been hidden from their sight by a wall of brilliant bougainvillea. The metal configuration of a tent, without the fabric of the tent itself, had instead been lavishly wrapped in huge magnolia flowers, which formed an integral cover of its own, while the roof was left open, filled only by hundreds of tiny white lights.

The tables were covered with antique white lace linen and set with antique silverware, floral cut-glass crystal, and candles set in crystal candelabras. Plates would be set upon sterling silver chargers, and the centerpieces were bowls of deep red roses. Placed on each white napkin was a menu card and a fragrant gardenia. The lighting was soft—mostly candlelight—and Italian singers sang lovely operatic arias during dinner.

Waiters, who had been selected for their Italian looks, served the meal, which began with an elaborate antipasto plate for each guest containing a variety of items, including a salad of baby arugula, prosciutto di Parma with shaved summer melon, and deep-fried artichoke hearts. Next came a pasta, tortellini with fresh porcini and Italian brown cremini mushrooms with a mascarpone cheese sauce, scattered with fresh peas, Italian parsley, basil, and thyme, served with a selection of homemade breads. And after an entrée of roasted sea bass or crusted lamb chops, and a pineapple sorbet to cleanse the palate, a dessert of wedding cake and chocolate groom's cake was served to each table. For the Italian touch, cannolis were made specially by Market. To top things off, there were handmade chocolate truffles and chocolate-dipped strawberries drizzled with white chocolate.

It was a sumptuous meal, which exhibited every outstanding quality Market consistently brings to the table: originality, versatility, organization, and awesome cuisine. But as Jena King puts it, perhaps their most important ingredient is one that cannot be bought. "I think they're phenomenal," she says, "because aside from everything else they do, they really care, and it shows."

# The Menu

## Tray-passed Hors D'oeuvres

### Tuscan Pizza

Topped with rosemary roasted potatoes and caramelized red onions melted with
Gorgonzola cheese

### Gamberoni Spiedini

Chargrilled shrimp skewers marinated with orange and fennel

### Melanzane

Grilled eggplant rolled with a goat cheese filling flavored with fresh basil, pancetta, and garlic

### Carpaccio

Thinly sliced seared beef tenderloin served on crostini with a light mustard sauce

### Chicken Liver Crostini

and

### Pomodoro Bruschetta

Vine-ripe red and yellow tomatoes grilled and drizzled lightly with extra virgin olive oil, fresh basil,
chopped shallots, and fragrant herbs

## Antipasti

# Insalata Arugula

Baby arugula salad drizzled with an oil and lemon dressing garnished with teardrop tomatoes with shaved parmigiano reggiano

# Prosciutto di Parma

With shaved summer melon and cracked black pepper

# Carciofi

Deep-fried artichoke hearts served with lemon wedges and fried parsley

# Fichi con Aceto Balsamico

Fresh figs drizzled with aged balsamic vinegar served with locatelli Romano cheese

## Pasta

# Tortellini ai Funghi

Fresh porcini and Italian brown cremini mushrooms with a mascarpone cheese sauce fragrant with fresh Italian parsley, basil, and thyme

## Entrée

### Branzino Arrosto

Roasted sea bass fillet marinated with fresh lemon and olive oil, topped with a warm salsa of sautéed
Italian tomatoes and onions, garlic, capers, sicilian olives, and fresh herbs.
Served with sautéed broccoli rapini and rosemary roasted potatoes

or

### Grilled Rack of Lamb with Garlic Mashed Potato Tower

Served with herb potato chips, caramelized pearl onions, sautéed red Swiss chard, french green
beans, red wine balsamic jus

with

Kalamata olive–caper cracker bread, ciabatta bread, grape and rosemary glazed focaccia,
black pepper brioche, round country style loaf,
served with sweet butter, replenished throughout the meal

### Pineapple Sorbet with Sweet Cherry Polenta Cookies

## Dessert

### Wedding Cake

and

### Chocolate Groom's Cake

### Handmade Chocolate Truffles
### Chocolate-dipped, Stemmed Strawberries Drizzled with White Chocolate
### Cannolis

# The Recipes

## Tuscan Pizza
(MAKES 3—4 12-INCH CRUSTS)

1 Tbs. yeast

1 pinch salt

1 Tbs. olive oil

3 cups all-purpose unbleached flour

1¼–1½ cups tepid (90°) water

Mix yeast and water together in a bowl to activate the yeast (5 minutes). Combine flour and salt in the bowl of a mixer fitted with a dough hook. Stir to incorporate. Add water with yeast to mixing bowl with olive oil. Mix at low speed to keep flour from scattering out of mixing bowl. Increase speed to medium as dough comes together. Continue to mix at medium speed 2—3 minutes or until dough forms a solid mass and begins to clean inside of bowl of all dried flour.

Turn dough out into a lightly oiled bowl, cover with plastic wrap, and allow to proof at room temperature until doubled in volume, about 1 hour. Cut risen dough into 3—4 even pieces on a floured surface and stretch each piece into a circle 9—10 inches in diameter.

Unbaked pizza crusts can be quick-frozen and wrapped to store up to one week in the freezer at this point. If using frozen crusts, lightly oil a 12-inch pizza pan; place frozen crust on pizza pan, covered with plastic wrap to thaw and proof (about ½ hour at room temperature).

Make a list of every item on the menu and which plates, platters, and utensils will be used to serve each item.

Make a list from the menu of every ingredient you will need to buy and how much of each is needed.

Assemble pizzas starting with a smear of roasted garlic, then cheese, then whatever toppings you choose. Bake in hot oven (450°) 10–12 minutes or until golden brown and bubbling.

### Suggested Toppings

ROASTED GARLIC: Cover peeled garlic cloves in olive oil with a scattering of fresh herbs and a bit of cracked black pepper in a small ovenproof pan. Bake at 275°–300° until garlic is golden brown and creamy soft. Roasted garlic can now be cooled and either left whole or pureed to be used in a number of ways to add a mild, sweet, nutty flavor to sauces, marinades, fillings, or in this case as a base for pizza toppings.

ROASTED TOMATOES: Halve and seed roma tomatoes, toss with olive oil, salt, and pepper, and roast in a slow oven (275°) 1–1½ hours or until most of tomato liquid has cooked off and skin easily peels away. Discard skin.

FRESH (BUFFALO) MOZZARELLA: It is always best to slice this cheese in advance and place on paper towels to absorb excess moisture to prevent soggy pizza crust.

ROSEMARY ROASTED RED POTATOES: Cut red jacket potatoes into small, ¼-inch dice; toss with olive oil, chopped rosemary, salt, and pepper. Spread on baking sheet and roast (375°) 10–20 minutes or until golden brown.

## Gamberoni Spiedini
Chargrilled Shrimp Marinated in Orange and Fennel
(SERVES 6)

12 large shrimp, peeled and
   deveined

1 cup fresh orange juice, reduced
   in a nonreactive pan to $^{1}/_{2}$ cup

$^{1}/_{4}$ cup extra virgin olive oil

$^{1}/_{2}$ Tbs. toasted fennel
   seeds, crushed

1 tsp. roasted garlic puree

Salt and pepper to taste

Mix all ingredients together, cover and marinate for at least 1 hour to fully develop flavor. Skewer on bamboo skewers or rosemary branches. Grill over medium-high heat 2 minutes per side or until firm. Serve immediately.

## Melanzane
Crisp Eggplant Rolled with Goat Cheese and Pancetta
(SERVES 6)

3 long straight Japanese egg-
   plants, sliced lengthwise $^{1}/_{4}$-inch

Olive oil

White pepper

3 oz. fresh goat cheese

1 Tbs. roasted garlic puree

3 leaves fresh basil, shredded fine

1 oz. minced pancetta (Italian
   style brine-cured bacon), sautéed

1 egg

1 cup flour

1 cup fresh toasted bread crumbs

Grapeseed oil for frying

Be organized. Knowing exactly what china and silver to use for each course in advance is important. Run through your event in your mind, visualize, and pretend you are a guest entering your home. Walk through the evening looking for areas of potential rough edges. Check that you've covered everything.

## Tips

Brush eggplant slices lightly with olive oil, sprinkle with white pepper, and sauté over medium heat until just soft. Spread out on a sheet pan to cool. Meanwhile, mix the goat cheese with the roasted garlic, basil, and pancetta. Check for seasoning, chill to firm up cheese, then form into small balls, about ³/₄ inch in diameter. Lay eggplant slice on work surface with larger end toward you. Place goat cheese ball on large end of eggplant slice and roll eggplant around cheese, covering the cheese completely. Roll eggplant balls in flour to coat; dip into egg mixture then into breadcrumbs to coat completely. If making these more than a day in advance to cooking, it is best to refrigerate eggplant rolls uncovered for about 2 hours to form a good dry crust on the outside to prevent them from sticking together. Deep fry $(350^\circ)$ in grapeseed oil until golden brown (2−3 minutes). Drain on paper towels before serving.

## Insalata Arugula
(SERVES 6)

**6 cups loosely packed arugula leaves**

**¹/₄ cup extra virgin olive oil**

**¹/₄ cup fresh squeezed lemon juice**

**1 basket sweet 100 tomatoes (tiny sweet cherry tomatoes)**

**¹/₂ cup parmigiano reggiano (thinly shaved with a vegetable peeler)**

Toss arugula with olive oil and lemon juice, place on plate, and garnish with tomatoes and shaved reggiano.

# Carciofi
Deep-Fried Artichoke Bottoms
(SERVES 6)

3 large artichokes, trimmed of all
   leaves, inner spines, and stem
   end (rub all over with lemon
   juice to prevent discoloring)
1/2 cup flour

1 lemon, cut into wedges, seeds
   removed
Flat leaf parsley tops
Grapeseed oil

Cut artichoke bottoms into 1/4-inch strips; immediately dredge in flour, drop into (350°) grapeseed oil, and fry to golden brown. Drain on paper towels and season with salt. Meanwhile, drop parsley into oil, fry 1 minute, drain on paper towel. This can be prepared in advance to this point, then placed in oven to reheat before serving. Place fried artichokes on plate next to arugula salad; garnish with lemon wedge and fried parsley.

# Fichi con Aceto Balsamico
(SERVES 6)

Cut a fresh fig in crisscross pattern 3/4 through, spread out and place a nice chunk of locatelli Romano cheese in the opening, drizzle with aged balsamic vinegar.

## Tips

Do whatever you can the day before the party: Set the table. Tape notes on your refrigerator to remind you what to do during the serving of the meal. Clear off the counter so you have plenty of space. Maximize your kitchen. Always stay organized throughout the dinner.

Make sure you have adequate help. The host really sets the tone. If you're too hurried and scurried, your nervousness will carry over. You should have a staff person for each 25 to 30 guests.

## Tips

Take care in planning your hors d'oeuvres. Don't feed people too much before dinner, and plan the entrée before you plan the hors d'oeuvres, so the entrée doesn't lose its appeal. Remember, less is more. If you're serving lots of courses, keep the portions small.

For a special touch, decorate the hors d'oeuvres tray with flowers like the ones used for the decor of the party.

## Tortellini ai Funghi

Tortellini Filled with Porcini and Italian Brown Cremini Mushrooms
(SERVES 6)

1.5 lb. fresh porcini mushrooms, sliced $1/4$ inch

1.5 lb. fresh cremini mushrooms, sliced $1/4$ inch

1 Tbs. freshly squeezed lemon juice

2 medium shallots, peeled and chopped fine

$1/2$ bunch flat leaf parsley, chopped

$1/2$ bunch basil, chopped

$1/2$ bunch thyme, chopped

$1/2$ bunch chives, chopped

1 pint ricotta cheese

2 eggs (one whipped to seal pasta, one for filling)

1 quart cream

1 cup white wine

1 pint mascarpone cheese

$1/4$ cup roasted garlic puree

$1/4$ cup parmigiano reggiano

1 recipe pasta dough, rolled thin and cut into 2-inch squares (or purchased fresh pasta sheets will work in a pinch)

Sauté mushrooms, shallots, and 1 Tbs. of each of the herbs in olive oil over medium-high heat about 5 minutes, sprinkling lemon juice in at the end, and set aside to cool. Meanwhile, reduce cream by half over low heat, being careful not to let it boil over. Add white wine, reduce by $1/3$, and add mascarpone, roasted garlic, and $1/2$ of mushroom mixture. Taste for seasoning.

In a medium bowl, mix ricotta, $1/2$ of mushrooms, 1 egg, salt, and pepper. Place 1 rounded spoonful of mixture in the center of each pasta square; brush $1/2$ of the pasta with whipped egg; fold in half, corner to corner; grab both ends of folded pasta sheet and

112

pinch together, sealing with a little more egg. Place on wire rack in your refrigerator to dry slightly (about 1 hour) then hold in the refrigerator, wrapped until ready to use. At this point, pasta can be put in the freezer to hold for up to 2 weeks; however it will be best served the same day that it is prepared.

Cook tortellini in salted water at a rolling boil, about 5 minutes. Drain, toss with the sauce adding a bit of pasta water if needed, place in pasta bowls, and sprinkle with some of the remaining herbs and reggiano.

## Grilled Rack of Lamb with Garlic Mashed Potato Tower
(SERVES 6)

### Lamb

3 frenched 1/2 racks of lamb

### Marinade

| | |
|---|---|
| 1/4 cup roasted garlic, pureed | 1 Tbs. soy sauce |
| 3–4 fresh basil leaves, chopped | Cracked black pepper |
| 1/2 cup extra virgin olive oil | |

Combine marinade ingredients in a small steel bowl and blend together. Rub each piece of lamb with the marinade, using all of it, and then place in a covered container. Refrigerate overnight or at least for 2 hours. About an hour before serving, place lamb on a medium-high grill, marking both sides for color, 1–2 minutes per side. Place lamb on a baking sheet to finish in a hot (400°) oven for 8 minutes, allowing a 10-minute resting period before slicing to serve.

*Tips*

Work with what you have. If you don't have room for a sit-down dinner, don't plan one; plan a buffet instead.

Organization is key. Write things down. First do a schedule: what time hors d'oeuvres will be passed; what time dinner will be served.

## Garlic Mashed Potatoes

| | |
|---|---|
| 3 medium russet potatoes, peeled and cut into 2-inch cubes | $^1/_4$–$^1/_2$ cup whole milk |
| 3 Tbs. unsalted butter | 2 Tbs. roasted garlic puree |
| | Salt and white pepper |

Place potatoes in a sauce pot and cover with water. Adding a pinch of salt, place potatoes on the stove and bring to a boil over high heat. Once the potatoes begin to boil, reduce heat to a low rolling simmer to ensure even cooking. Boil until a small knife can easily be inserted into the potatoes—15 to 20 minutes. Drain potatoes into a colander, shaking off any excess liquid. Place into a bowl of a mixer fitted with a whip attachment; add butter, milk, and roasted garlic. Turn on machine briefly, just enough to incorporate the ingredients and form a smooth puree. Season to taste with salt and white pepper. Be careful not to overwhip the potatoes or they will become gummy.

NOTE: Potatoes can be cooked and cooled in advance, then heated to serve without any loss in taste.

Be a guest at your party. Have fun by preparing as much in advance as possible, so you have only to finish dishes and last-minute touches when needed. This will increase your enjoyment of entertaining and make your guests feel relaxed and more at home.

Create an ambience with dim lights and a fire in winter. Nice soft background music enhances and accents the food.

## Caramelized Pearl Onions

| | |
|---|---|
| 24 pearl onions, peeled | 2 Tbs. sugar |
| 2 Tbs. canola oil | 1/2 cup water |
| 1 tsp. ground cumin | |

Heat canola oil in a medium sauté pan over medium heat. Add onions and sauté about 5 minutes, shaking the pan until the onions are evenly golden. Add sugar and cumin, then the water over the onions, tossing to incorporate for an additional 5 minutes, or until the onions are cooked through and well glazed. Season with salt and pepper to taste. Keep warm or reheat to serve later.

## Balsamic Jus

| | |
|---|---|
| 1/4 lb. button mushrooms, chopped | 1 1/2 cup good red wine (preferably what is served with dinner) |
| 1 large onion | |
| 1 1/2 lb. lamb bones and scraps cut in 2-inch pieces (from your butcher) | 6 cup veal stock |
| | 1/4 cup imported balsamic vinegar |
| A handful of parsley stems, thyme, bay leaf | |

Place bones and scraps of lamb in a heavy-bottomed saucepan over medium heat. Add chopped mushrooms, onion, and herbs. Sauté 5 minutes, releasing aroma and coloring the ingredients in your pan. Add wine and bring to a boil, reducing the heat, simmering gently until reduced to almost dry. Add the stock. Simmer about 1 hour, or until liquid is reduced to about 2 cups. Add balsamic vinegar and cook 2 minutes. Remove from heat and strain through a fine mesh strainer, discarding all of the solids. Season to taste with salt and pepper. Keep warm to serve or rewarm later.

## Veal Stock

| | |
|---|---|
| 1/4 cup canola oil | I cup canned tomato puree |
| 7 lbs. veal shank bones (ask your butcher) | 3 sprigs thyme |
| | 8 peppercorns |
| 3 onions, 2 carrots, I cup celery, all chopped | I bay leaf |

Oil bones; place in roasting pan in 375 ° oven 20–40 minutes or until well browned. Place bones in stockpot. Add remaining ingredients to roasting pan and place over medium heat on stovetop for 5 minutes or until softened. Transfer to stockpot.

Add 2 cups water to roasting pan and cook, scraping up any particles stuck to pan, about 2 minutes or until the pan is deglazed. Pour into stockpot. Add 3 quarts water or unsalted chicken stock to stockpot. Bring to a boil over medium-high heat, skimming the surface of foam. Reduce heat to a simmer and cook for 6 hours, skimming as the stock cooks.

When strained this recipe should yield 6 cups veal stock.

Lili Goldstein McLean, Jeff McLean, and Robin Goldstein

# PATINA CATERING

## Joachim & Christine Splichal, Stephanie Edens & Jon Ternow

"WHAT SETS US APART IS the creativity of our food. We believe creativity in cooking is key."

# The Affair

## Spirit of Life Dinner/City of Hope

The award-winning restaurant Patina is, quite simply, in a class by itself. Widely known and appreciated for world-renowned master chef and restaurateur Joachim Splichal's highly regarded cuisine, it has been named the best restaurant in Los Angeles for the last seven years by the notable Zagat survey. Splichal has cooked for everyone from Bill Clinton, Ronald Reagan, Margaret Thatcher, Henry Kissinger, and George Bush to Warren Beatty, Tom Hanks, and Holly Hunter.

The loyalty he commands—atypical of a town in which tastes in everything from fashion to food change faster than movie box-office grosses—is precisely what propelled Splichal to dive into the business of catering. Patina's clientele demanded no less than the excellence and creativity to which they had become so accustomed at the restaurant for those special occasions on which they wanted to entertain at home. Thus what began six years ago with a few intimate dinners at private homes today has grown into a $3 million-a-year catering business, adding the special Patina flair to events including the prime-time Emmy Awards, movie premieres, and corporate events as well as the matchless intimate private dinners that originally launched Patina into catering.

Wherever the event takes place, the lofty standards set by the prized restaurant prevail. "We take the look and the style of Patina with us always," says Patina Catering's director, Stephanie Edens. "There's no doubt about it; we always strive for understated elegance, fabulous food, and excellent service." These same ingredients are present in all of the restaurants in Splichal's growing California empire: Pinot Bistro in Studio City; Cafe Pinot in downtown Los Angeles; Pinot at the Chronicle in Pasadena; Pinot Blanc in Napa Valley; Pinot Provence in Costa Mesa; and Patinette, the lunch cafe at the Museum of Contemporary Art in Los Angeles.

Anyone who attended the 1997 Spirit of Life Dinner, which is the music and entertainment industry's annual benefit for the City of Hope, will unequivocally agree that Patina Catering's winning formula prevailed, as always. The spectacular affair turned out precisely as it had been planned—not only understated and elegant, but eminently successful as well, raising more than $3 million for the charity.

The evening commenced with a cocktail reception. When guests—among them honorees Kenneth "Babyface" Edmonds and Antonio "L.A." Reid, along with other luminaries including Shaquille O'Neal and singer Toni Braxton—arrived, they sipped cocktails (there was plenty of fine champagne) and enjoyed some of Patina Catering's unique tray-passed hors d'oeuvres: Baked French Fries with Garlic Dip; Lobster, Green Apple, and Mint served in a spoon in classic Patina style; Polenta Fritters with Dungeness Crab, Roasted Corn, and Bell Peppers; Crispy Pita Chip with Shredded Lamb and Feta Cheese; and Stuffed Oven-dried Tomato with Sweet Garlic Mousse.

Everything Patina Catering prepared for the evening had been created specially for the gala, in keeping with Splichal's culinary philosophy: "What sets you apart from everyone else is the quality of the food and the ingenuity of the food." After devising a number of potential items for each course and brainstorming with Edens and catering chef Jon Fernow about the logistics of the event, Splichal decided on the final menu with the consensus of the client. The entrée would be Seared Whitefish with Corn and Winter Squash, served with Chive Sauce, preceded by a Salad of Haricots Verts with Mango, Shrimp, and Baby Mixed Greens. And for dessert, a delectable pastry: a Lemon Macaroon with Mint Chocolate Sauce and Caramelized Citrus.

The setting for the affair was exquisite, yet understated. The dinner for 1,500 was served in a free-span tent, completely transparent on every side to give the room a very open feeling. An amethyst-colored carpet covered the floor, and each of the 150 tables had tablecloths of a shimmering, almost luminescent taffeta-like fabric that radiated tones of beautiful deep purple. The centerpieces realized the same refined style: On each table, five oversized hurricane lamps containing large, glimmering church candles accented the clear china, simple black napkins, cylindrical glasses, and hammer-patterned silverware.

After a perfectly orchestrated and incomparable meal, the guests of honor received their awards, and Toni Braxton topped off the evening with a glorious performance. One guest summed the evening up well: "Patina Catering takes everything to a higher level, a whole other plane. That's what makes the restaurant, and everything it touches, so special."

# The Menu

**Tray-passed Hors D'oeuvres**

Baked French Fries with Garlic Dip

Lobster, Green Apple & Mint
Served in a spoon

Polenta Fritters with Dungeness Crab,
Roasted Corn & Bell Peppers

Crispy Pita Chip
with Shredded Lamb and Feta Cheese

Stuffed Oven-dried Tomato with Sweet Garlic Mousse

**First Course**

Salad of Haricots Verts with Mango, Shrimp
& Baby Mixed Greens

**Entrée**

Seared Whitefish
with Corn and Winter Squash
Served with Chive Sauce

Vegetarian Alternate
Pennini with Roasted Artichokes, Grilled Radicchio,
Corn, Winter Squash & Plum Tomatoes

Assorted Bread, Rolls, Foccacia & Breadsticks
Served with sweet butter

**Dessert**

Lemon Macaroon
with Mint Chocolate Sauce and Caramelized Citrus

Assorted Cookies & Biscotti
Served at each table

Freshly Brewed Regular & Decaffeinated Coffees
Hot Tea

# The Recipes

## Salad of Haricots Verts, Mango, Shrimp & Baby Mixed Greens
(SERVES 4)

12 ¹⁶/₂₀ (large) shrimp, cooked
   and peeled

3 cups haricots verts (French
   green beans)

1 mango

2 roma tomatoes, peeled and cut
   into strips

1 shallot, chopped

2 Tbs. basil chiffonade

2 cups baby mixed greens

### Vinaigrette

Juice of 2 lemons

Juice of 1 orange

1 cup olive oil

Salt and pepper to taste

To make the vinaigrette, squeeze the 2 lemons and the 1 orange. Place the juice in a medium-sized mixing bowl, then using a whisk add the olive oil slowly and finish with salt and pepper.

   To prepare the haricots verts first remove both ends of the beans and blanch in boiling salted water till tender. Cool the beans off in ice water after cooking.

   To prepare the roma tomato strips, you must first remove the skin of the tomato by placing the tomatoes in boiling water for 5 seconds, removing and then quickly placing in ice water. Remove the skin by using a paring knife. Make one cut lengthwise on each tomato and remove the center, leaving only the outer skin. Cut the outer skin into ¼-inch strips.

## Tips

Make the most of your home. Use different areas for different portions of the event: Have cocktails in the living room, dinner in the dining room, dessert on the terrace, or utilize whatever space you have.

Create an ambience in your home to compliment the mood of your event: formally attired staff and dim lights for formal affairs, upbeat music and a fun menu for an afternoon barbecue.

To prepare the mango, remove the skin and cut the flesh from the pit. Then cut the flesh into a medium-sized dice, about $1/2$-inch square.

To assemble the plate toss the baby mixed greens with just a touch of citrus vinaigrette and place in the middle of the salad plate. Next mix the haricots verts, mango dice, tomato strips, shallots, basil, and citrus vinaigrette; finish with salt and pepper as needed. Place this mixture in equal amounts on top of the mixed greens and top it with 3 pieces of shrimp.

## Vegetable Nage

| | |
|---|---|
| 1 Tbs. unsalted butter | 1 sprig fresh thyme |
| 10 ribs celery, coarsely chopped | 6 cloves unpeeled garlic |
| 1 large white onion, coarsely chopped | 1 sprig fresh parsley |
| | 1 quart white wine |
| 2 leeks, white part only, coarsely chopped | 1 quart water |

This recipe yields a half quart of vegetable stock. In order to make the finished butter nage, you will need only 5 oz. of the stock. The remaining stock can be chilled for up to 3 days, or if you like, frozen in 5-oz. quantities for future sauces.

In a large saucepan, melt the butter over low heat and add the vegetables and herbs. Sweat the mixture over medium-low heat, stirring occasionally, for about 30 minutes, or until the vegetables are completely translucent and almost broken down. Be sure not to let them brown at all; otherwise the sauce will not be perfectly white. Add wine, increase heat slightly, and simmer gently for 1 hour. Add the water and simmer gently for an additional 20 minutes. Strain the stock through a sieve, pressing down hard on the solids to be sure you extract all the flavor from them. Discard the vegetables and set the stock aside. Measure $2/3$ cup stock into a medium saucepan, and chill or freeze the remaining stock.

# Finished Butter Nage
(SERVES 4)

$2/3$ cup vegetable stock

$3/4$ cup unsalted butter at room temperature, cut into six equal pieces

Salt and freshly ground white pepper

At serving time, when you are ready to finish the nage, bring the stock to a boil, then reduce the heat to low. Add $1/3$ of the butter, stir until melted, then pour the nage into a blender. Blend at high speed, removing the lid to gradually add the remaining 4 pieces of butter, and blend just until thoroughly emulsified. Season to taste with salt and pepper, and use as directed in the recipe. Use within an hour. To reheat if cold, bring the nage back to a simmer and blend again for 10 to 15 seconds to re-emulsify.

# Seared Whitefish with Corn & Winter Squash, Served with Chive Sauce
(SERVES 4)

4 whitefish fillets, about
   5$^1$/2 oz. each

Flour as needed

4 cups fresh yellow corn off the cob
   (frozen corn may also be used)

1 cup sweet potato dice,
   $^1$/4" x $^1$/4"

$^1$/2 cup heavy cream

$^1$/4 cup unsalted butter

$^1$/2 cup raw nage (see Vegetable
   Nage, above)

$^1$/4 cup chopped chives

$^1$/2 lb. pea shoots

Salt and pepper as needed

To make the corn and sweet potato mixture for under the fish, first you have to roast the yellow corn. Use a hot sauté pan, add a touch of oil, and then add the corn. Sauté the corn until lightly golden brown and tender. Puree the corn by roughly chopping it and adding it to a Cuisinart. Cut the sweet potatoes into $\frac{1}{4}$-inch dice; season lightly with salt, pepper, and olive oil; and roast the potatoes in a 350° oven until tender. To finish the mixture, put the chopped corn, the roasted corn, and the roasted sweet potatoes together in a pan and slowly heat up with the butter and heavy cream. The mixture should be fairly thick in consistency. Finish with salt, pepper, and half of the chopped chives.

To make the sauce, blend the raw nage in a blender, adding the whole butter. The sauce should have a fairly thick consistency. Add the other half of the chives to the sauce when you are ready to put the food on the plate.

To sear off the whitefish, first dust the skin lightly with flour, then sauté with a touch of oil until the skin is golden brown and the fish is cooked.

To cook the pea shoots, you can either sauté them with a touch of butter or steam them in a steamer.

To assemble the plate, first put the corn and sweet potato mixture down on the middle of the plate, topped with the pea shoots. Next, place the whitefish on top of the pea shoots and finish with the chive sauce around the fish.

## Lemon Macaroon with Mint Chocolate Sauce & Caramelized Citrus
(SERVES 6)

### Macaroons

| | |
|---|---|
| 4 oz. powdered sugar | 2 1/8 oz. egg white |
| 2 1/8 oz. ground almonds | 5/8 oz. granulated sugar |

Sift powdered sugar and ground almonds through a sifter. Whip egg whites with sugar to a soft meringue. Fold the powdered sugar–almond mixture gently into the meringue. Pipe circles (3 inches in diameter) onto parchment, and bake at 325° until golden brown. Makes about 12 pieces.

## Tips

Provide guests with a party gift that is connected to the event, such as a recipe for one of the dishes served, a CD of the music played, or cookies served along with dessert.

## Filling

| | |
|---|---|
| ¹/₂ lb. granulated sugar | 3 egg yolks |
| ¹/₂ cup lemon juice | 1 Tbs. lemon zest |
| 3 whole eggs | 6 oz. butter |

Put all ingredients into a bowl, and cook over a double boiler until mixture thickens. Strain the lemon curd through cheese-cloth and chill in refrigerator. Pipe lemon curd in between two macaroons so it looks like a sandwich or hamburger.

## Chocolate Sauce

| | |
|---|---|
| 2 cups water | 7 oz. bitter chocolate |
| 7 oz. granulated sugar | Mint liqueur |

Bring water to a boil. Pour over chopped chocolate and stir until dissolved. Add mint liqueur to taste.

## Caramelized Citrus

| | |
|---|---|
| 2 pink grapefruit | 1 lime |
| 4 oranges | 1 pound granulated sugar |
| 1 lemon | 2 cups water |

Peel the skin off the fruit and cut into segments. Bring water to a boil, add sugar, and continue to cook until it gets a nice caramel color. Add fruit segments to warm caramel sauce and let soak for about an hour.

TO ASSEMBLE: Arrange macaroon on plate. Arrange caramelized citrus pieces around the macaroon. Drizzle chocolate sauce on plate.

Chef Jon Fernow, Christine Splichal, Joachim Splichal, and Stephanie Edens

*Caterer to the Stars—and Pols:*

A dinner for Ronald Reagan, George Bush, Mikhail Gorbachev, and Margaret Thatcher at the Fairmont Hotel in San Francisco.

A special meal for Bill Clinton and a Democratic fundraiser.

A kosher dinner for Leah Rabin, for which Splichal brought in rabbis to bless his kitchen.

Holly Hunter's wedding

The Emmy Awards party for 4,000 people

# SPAGO

## *Wolfgang Puck*

**W**HEN OUR CUSTOMERS AT SPAGO & CHINOIS WALK THROUGH THE DOOR, THEY ARE GREETED BY LARGE, STUNNING FLORAL ARRANGEMENTS. To start the evening on such a note is to be filled with optimism for what lies ahead. In the same way, the appetizer acts as a spectacular entrance into the meal. I cannot overemphasize the importance of a good start.

# The Fire and Ice Ball

It has arguably become the most coveted ticket in Hollywood, which is one reason that the star-studded, fourth annual Fire and Ice Ball, a stunning black-tie gala in which Hollywood joins forces with the elite of the fashion world to raise money for women's cancer research at UCLA, was sold out before the invitations even hit the mail. Underwritten by Revlon, the affair has become an intensely sought-after showcase for New York fashion designers, and this year's featured designer was Isaac Mizrahi, who unveiled his newest collection.

Chaired by Lily Tartikoff, whose husband, Brandon, had died of cancer earlier in the year, along with the combined forces of Ben Bourgeois productions, which produced the gala, and Spago Catering, with the inimitable Wolfgang Puck at the helm, the event lived up to its reputation. With a dazzling celebrity guest list that included Tom Hanks and his wife, Rita Wilson, Dustin and Lisa Hoffman, Anjelica Huston, Sidney Poitier, Cindy Crawford, and many of Hollywood's top moguls, the evening was a smashing success—easily, many would say, as sensational as a major Hollywood production.

But decide for yourself. Had you attended, your experience would have been something like this: At around 7:30 P.M. your limo drives you up to a curving ramp, which leads to an immense white tent that appears to be floating on a glistening sea. As you proceed, wondrous fountains spewing fire and water, interspersed among hundreds of floating candles, light up the air around you. You are actually at Paramount Studios, and the million-gallon water tank that you are now walking over was once the Red Sea in the film *The Ten Commandments*. As you enter the tent's reception area, waiters in formal attire pass trays of Wolfgang Puck's trademark pizzas, and cocktails are being served from an illuminated Plexiglas bar, backed by a wall made of 15,000 pounds of ice. Flanking it on each side is a video screen. You look up, and stare into the eyes of a mélange of brilliantly colored tropical fish, as though you were underwater.

Across the room, you notice something else astounding: A thin sheet of rain has been created to form a veritable wall of water that separates the cocktail area from what is beyond it. Within moments, like the Red Sea, the water will part, signaling it is time to enter the dining area. You move to the next room, stepping onto a clear Plexiglas runway extending the 160-foot length of the room. It glimmers brilliantly as the lights from above bounce off a thousand pounds of broken mirrors that have been sunk beneath the water's surface.

The tables for the sit-down dinner for 1,200 guests are terraced on each side, so every diner will have an unobstructed view of the evening's much-anticipated fashion show. You marvel at the simplicity of the table's elegant decor: crisp white cotton linen napkins and tablecloths to the floor, sterling silver chargers, and hand-blown Judel glasses. The tables are lit with lamps—frosted Plexiglas cylinders designed by Mizrahi himself—each wired on an individual dimmer. Around each cylinder are five clusters of pink and white peonies.

Meanwhile, back in the enormous kitchen, which has been built in a separate tent expressly for this event, Wolfgang Puck is busy overseeing the preparation of the meal. In keeping with his inimitable style, it will be simple and hearty, yet elegant: roasted salmon, Puck's famous mashed potatoes, a Cabernet sauce, and a medley of seasonal vegetables and dessert, all of which will be served by the 280 waiters standing at the ready until the pre-dinner program is completed.

You are seated comfortably at your table of 10 guests as the program begins. Tom Hanks and Rita Wilson are the hosts, having stepped in for Tom Cruise and Nicole Kidman, whose film project in England has delayed their intended return for the Ball. Still, Cruise and Kidman appear in a short video with a message of thanks to the audience, followed by short speeches by Paramount executive Sherry Lansing and others. And then, after a touching video of Brandon Tartikoff, Lily Tartikoff stands at the podium and delivers a heart-wrenching tribute, provoking tears among the audience.

The somber mood changes when Mizrahi's fashion show begins, and the room becomes electric once more, reaching a climax as models clad only in their underwear pass through another wall of water. The dinner lives up to Puck's stellar reputation, and plenty of Hollywood shmoozing continues well into the night. When it is finally time to go home, there is not an iota of doubt about it: The Fire and Ice Ball has not disappointed. It has been, yet again, an affair to remember.

# *The Menu*

## Tray-passed Hors D'oeuvres

Pizza with Smoked Salmon and Dill Cream

Pizza with Grilled Vegetables (some without cheese)

Spicy Shrimp Pizza

Duck Sausage Pizza

Wild Mushroom Pizza

## Entrée

Frisée & Spinach Salad with Baby Beets, Goat Cheese & Toasted Walnuts

Roasted Salmon with a Black Pepper & Ginger Crust

Horseradish Mashed Potatoes

& Cabernet Sauce

with

Baby Carrots & Green Beans

Homemade Breads (Including Matzo) & Butter

## Dessert

French Butter Apple Tart with Caramel Ice Cream

Platters of Petit Sweets

Coffee & Tea

# The Recipes

## Roasted Salmon with a Black Pepper & Ginger Crust
(SERVES 6)

6 salmon filets, about 7 oz. each

¹/₄ cup clarified butter

¹/₄ cup chopped ginger

2 Tbs. crushed black pepper

Salt to taste

Brush salmon with butter lightly, dust with ginger and black pepper, and bake until pink in the middle.

## Horseradish Mashed Potatoes

10 100-count Idaho potatoes

1 gallon salted water

2 cups heavy cream

¹/₄ cup butter

¹/₃ cup freshly grated horseradish

Salt and pepper to taste

Peel potatoes, cut in sixths, start in cold salted water, and bring up to a boil. Reduce to a simmer, cook until skewer tender, strain, and put through potato ricer. Add warm cream, soft butter, horseradish, and salt and pepper to taste.

## Cabernet Sauce

Olive oil as needed

1/2 cup smashed ginger

1/4 cup chopped garlic

2 cups sliced shallots

1 bunch thyme

Crushed black pepper

1/4 gallon red wine

1/2 gallon port wine

2 cups veal stock

2 cups chicken stock

1/2 cup whole butter

Salt and pepper to taste

Sweat ginger, garlic, and shallots in olive oil until caramelized. Add thyme and black pepper, deglaze with red wine and port, reduce to syrup, add veal and chicken stock, and reduce by 2/3. Strain, whisk in 1/2 cup whole butter. Season with salt and pepper to taste.

## Frisée & Spinach Salad with Baby Beets, Goat Cheese & Toasted Walnuts

2 heads frisée (white leaves only)

1/2 lb. baby spinach

1/4 lb. baby arugula

5 baby beets cut in quarters

20 walnuts*

3 oz. goat cheese

4 oz. citrus vinaigrette

Arrange beets, goat cheese, and walnuts on plate. Mix lettuce with dressing, season with salt and pepper.

*For candied walnuts, blanch nuts in boiling water for one minute, drain, toss with confectioners' sugar until sugar becomes translucent, fry in 350° oil for 1-2 minutes until golden brown, and cool on sheet pan.

**Citrus Shallot Vinaigrette**

| | |
|---|---|
| 1 1/2 quarts orange juice | Orange zest |
| 1/3 cup chopped shallots | 1 cup hazelnut oil |
| 2 Tbs. chopped thyme | 1 cup olive oil |
| 1/2 cup balsamic vinegar | Salt and pepper to taste |

Reduce orange juice down to 1 1/2 cups, cool down, add shallots, thyme, balsamic, orange zest, and slowly season with salt and pepper.

# French Butter Apple Tart

Courtesy of Sherry Yard, Pastry Chef, Spago
(SERVES 8)

6 apples (pick your favorite: Jonagolds, Crispins, or Granny Smiths)

8 4-inch puff pastry circles

1 cup applesauce

1/2 of frangipange (see recipe below)

Place the pre-cut puff pastry circles on parchment. Spread a thin layer of frangipange on bottom. Smear applesauce on top. Fan the apples in desired design. Brush with butter, then lightly dust with sugar. Bake at 375° for 10 minutes, then turn the oven down to 325° and continue to bake until dark golden and no white dough can be seen. Top with apple caramel and dust with powdered sugar.

## Caramelized Apple Compote Filling for French Butter Apple Tart

| | |
|---|---|
| 6 apples | $^1/_4$ cup heavy cream |
| 1 oz. butter | $^1/_3$ cup lemon juice |
| 1 vanilla bean | $^1/_3$ cup brandy |
| $^1/_2$ cup sugar | |

Peel, core, and cut apples into 1-inch pieces. Over a moderate flame, add butter to a medium-size saucepan. Bring to noisette. Add the sugar and allow to caramelize. Just when you think it is going to burn, add the apples. Add the brandy, and sauté for 3–5 minutes until tender. Add to food processor and pulse until smooth puree. Cool down and refrigerate until ready to use.

## Frangipange Filling
(Bottom layer for French Butter Apple Tart)

| | |
|---|---|
| 6 oz. butter | 4 eggs |
| 7 oz. almond paste | 4 oz. cake flour |
| 6 oz. sugar | 1 Tbs. Sambucca |

Cream together the butter and the sugar with the almond paste and optional lemon zest. Cream with a paddle attachment in the mixing bowl. Add the eggs one at a time, scraping down as you go. Add the Sambucca to the flour.

# SUDANO'S

*Ian Sudano*

"A LOT OF PEOPLE IN HOLLY-WOOD HAVE STARTED TO UNDERSTAND THAT OVER-OPULENT IS NOT NECESSARILY GOOD. If you do things very tastefully you can have all the finest things and yet never be pretentious in any way."

# The Affair

## An Intimate Backyard Party

There is a certain special feeling that permeates every affair created by Ian Sudano. It is an absolute sense of beauty and well-being, undoubtedly derived from the unique combination of his genteel South African background, so profusely influenced by worldly sensibilities, and his calm, creative, capable mien, enhanced by such a giving and loving nature that it cannot help but shine through everything he does. Which is at least partially why the birthday party Sudano did recently for a well-known actor at his L.A. home seemed to have a positively otherworldly glow.

It was a lovely autumn evening, and in keeping with Sudano's philosophy of "less is more," the style of the night was a delectable mixture of taste, simplicity, and warmth. The actor's wife, a professor, worked closely with Sudano to help him execute her vision of what she wanted her husband's birthday party to be. She had worked with Sudano before, and he understood her personal predilections. "She has very specific feelings about things like flowers and color combinations," Sudano explains. "She likes her flowers to be very artful and beautiful, and extremely fresh. And I know what her taste is, when it comes to a meal. It is the same as mine: it has to be great food, very beautifully presented, excellent staff, and efficient service." Their efforts melded for the perfect outcome.

When guests arrived, hors d'oeuvres were served inside the warm, inviting home, where lovely bouquets of tulips, lilies, and water lilies accented the baroque decor. As trays of Tuna Tartar on a Crostini, Endive Spears with a Dollop of Vegetable Caponata, Lime-marinated Shrimp with Tomato Cilantro Relish, California Sushi Rolls with a Wasabi Soy Dipping Sauce, and Walnut Shortbread with Pear and Blue Cheese were passed by white-coated waiters, a pianist played and sang softly, creating a welcoming and alluring atmosphere.

After cocktails, the diners proceeded through a lovely covered patio, the terra-cotta floor of which had been covered for the evening with Persian rugs, out to the grassy, lushly landscaped back-yard. "When there's no room as such and you're working with an open area, you need to create the ambience," says Sudano, "a look on the table that is warm and inviting for people to sit down."

Warm and inviting it was. The tables for the sit-down dinner were covered with copper cloths, and accented by black chairs and napkins. In keeping with the simple, outdoorsy feeling of the home as well as the dinner atmosphere, terra-cotta vases were used for the centerpieces, packed with rich roses and hydrangeas of deep, luscious colors—reds, dark reds, and dark purples—accented by fruits dripping from the lavish bouquets. A veritable sea of votive candles glistened about the flowers at each table. To complete the irresistible feeling, mellifluous music from a jazz string quartet joined by the pianist from earlier in the evening drifted from a balcony overlooking the yard.

It seemed to be the perfect birthday party. Good wine, good food, good feeling, and good wishes all flowed abundantly as the diverse mix of the couples' friends from the worlds of academia and acting meshed perfectly to make an exceptional group of guests. They were served their choice of Sudano's famous Crispy Salmon on a Bed of Jerusalem Artichoke Puree or Rack of Lamb on a Bed of Mashed Potatoes, then a Marjolaine birthday cake was presented to the birthday boy.

It was a lovely affair, one of ultimate quality, in keeping with Sudano's belief that quality and style are remembered long after everything else is forgotten. "You cannot," he insists, "accept anything that is less than perfect."

# The Menu

## Tray-passed Hors D'oeuvres

Tuna Tartar on a Crostini

Endive Spears with a Dollop of Vegetable Caponata

Lime-marinated Shrimp with Tomato Cilantro Relish

California Sushi Rolls with a Wasabi Soy Dipping Sauce

Walnut Shortbread with Pear & Blue Cheese

## First Course

Couscous Salad with Roasted Beets, Olives, Watercress
& Mint in a Light Lemon Vinaigrette

or

Roasted Fennel & Pear Salad
with a Champagne Pear Vinaigrette

## Sudano's Suggestions

When it comes to the cocktail hour, keep it at that. Anything longer than an hour becomes boring. In fact, 45 minutes is better.

Opulent is not necessarily good. Remember, "less is more." Quality and style are remembered long after everything else is forgotten.

Be creative when it comes to recipes. Pick a dish from your favorite restaurant and adapt it to your tastes.

Use hot plates for a hot meal, chilled forks for a salad. A hot meal should be served hot and a cold meal should be served cold. Otherwise, it will not be enjoyable.

## *Sudano's Suggestions*

Incorporate the character of the host into the party. If you are the host, your character should shine through.

When planning a party, the first thing to understand is exactly what the essence of the party is. Have an idea in your own mind of what you want the party to be. Understand your budget limitations. Create a menu that is reasonable within your budget to allow for other special touches, such as candles and flowers, in addition to the food.

The three most important ingredients for a successful event are simplicity, elegance, and above all, excellent, incredible food.

### Entrée

Rack of Lamb with a Wild Mushroom Sauce
Served on a Bed of Mashed Potatoes,
with Steamed Asparagus & Glazed Carrots

or

Crispy Salmon on a Bed of Jerusalem Artichoke Puree
Served with a Summer Vegetable Medley & Sautéed Spinach

### Dessert

Marjolaine Cake Served with Fruit Sorbets

### Coffee Service

Coffee Service Served with Champagne Truffles

## *Sudano's Suggestions*

When it comes to decor, use what you have within your own home. Build the shape of a table around the shape of a vase, a round table for round vessels, a square table for square ones. Mix table shapes if you require more than one table for seating, and use interesting touches, such as antique linens, if you have them.

Make the party easy and accessible for your guests to enjoy. Remember that people start feeling the flow of the party from the minute the invitation arrives and continue until they're ready to leave.

Don't try to substitute cocktails for dinner. Better to have a modest dinner than a million hors d'oeuvres. People who come at mealtime expect a meal.

# *The Recipes*

## Tuna Tartar on a Crostini
(YIELD: 25 CROSTINI)

### Crostini
Thinly sliced French baguette brushed with olive oil and fresh herbs (to include garlic). Toast until golden brown.

### Tuna Tartar

| | |
|---|---|
| ¹/₂ lb. tuna | I Tbs. olive oil |
| 2 roma tomatoes, diced | I Tbs. lime juice |
| ¹/₄ cup Bermudo onion, diced | I tsp. cayenne pepper |
| 2 Tbs. capers | Salt and pepper |
| 2 Tbs. parsley, chopped | |

Mix together finely diced tuna, seedless roma tomatoes, chopped capers, chopped parsley, and Bermuda onion. Just before serving, add olive oil, lime juice, cayenne pepper, and salt and pepper to taste.

## Endive Spears with a Dollop of Vegetable Caponata

| | |
|---|---|
| 2 bunches endive | I large carrot |
| 3 eggplants, sliced | 4 Tbs. onion, diced |
| 8 zucchini, sliced | 12 Kalamata olives, diced |
| 12 mushrooms | |

Clean endive and cut individual spears approximately 3 inches long. Grill assorted vegetables, including eggplant, zucchini, mushroom, onion, and carrot. Finely chop grilled vegetables and kalamata olives and combine. Place a dollop of mix on endive spear and serve.

154

## Lime-marinated Shrimp

Take dried whole large Mexican chilis, ground with lime juice and black pepper, and marinate shrimp for 10 minutes. Sauté in hot canola oil with a touch of sesame oil until cooked.

## Walnut Shortbread with Pear & Blue Cheese

Either make shortbread cookies with chopped walnuts or purchase. Thinly slice bosc pears into a fan with the peel. Place a slice of blue cheese on the cracker and fan the pear over the blue cheese.

## Couscous Salad with Roasted Beets, Olives, Watercress & Mint in a Light Lemon Vinaigrette
(SERVES 6–8)

| | |
|---|---|
| 1 package Couscous | 1/2 cup green olives |
| Milk | 1/2 cup black olives |
| Chicken stock | Watercress and mint leaves |
| 5 beets | |

Boil Couscous in milk and chicken stock (half and half, to yield amount of liquid called for on box) until cooked. Allow to cool. Oven roast whole beets at 375° until soft. Allow to cool.

To assemble salad, thinly slice beets into matchstick sizes. Chop green and black olives. Mix together. Add lemon vinaigrette (just enough to make couscous stick). Beets will color the couscous pink. Mold using a molding ring or a cup measure. Place on plate. Garnish the top of salad with a sprig of mint and sprinkle plate with finely chopped watercress leaves.

*Sudano's Suggestions*

Dessert is sometimes the most important part of the meal because it is one thing people don't eat every day. So do something interesting. Choose one dessert that can be the focus—like a special cake—made by either yourself or the baker, and surround it with some cookies and brownies and fruit. Remember cookies can be made ahead of time and frozen if you keep them in well-sealed containers, and brownie batter can be frozen before being baked. Thaw it and pop the brownies in the oven to bake the day of the party. Your guests will be impressed.

## Lemon Vinaigrette

| | |
|---|---|
| 2 Tbs. lemon juice | 3/4 cup olive oil |
| 2 Tbs. balsamic vinegar | Salt and freshly ground pepper |
| 1 Tbs. Dijon mustard | |

In a small bowl, whisk together lemon juice, vinegar, and mustard. Gradually add the oil, beating with a whisk until combined. Season with salt and pepper to taste.

# Crispy Salmon on a Bed of Jerusalem Artichoke Puree

Marinate the salmon in olive oil and dill, then cut into 8 oz. slices, and grill, skin side down, for 15 minutes, then turn just to mark the other side. Serve on top of artichoke puree.*

*AHEAD-OF-TIME NOTE: You can crisp your salmon on one side only, and set it aside covered. It can be finished in the oven for 10 minutes before you are ready to serve it.

## Artichoke Puree

Boil artichokes in water, white wine, and fresh herbs. Use 8–12 artichokes for puree to serve with 4 pieces of salmon. Peel artichokes, take out hearts, puree hearts, and reheat over a double boiler when ready to serve.

*Option note: You can add some mashed potato to the artichoke puree. It will feed more people and will be less expensive than using only artichokes, and it is not as rich.

# Index